WALKING DEV

THL
RIVER OTTER

Richard Easterbrook
&
Geoff Broadhurst

EASTERHURST PUBLICATIONS LTD

Photographs by Richard Easterbrook
Sketches by Geoff Broadhurst

ISBN 0 9538272 1 6
© Richard Easterbrook & Geoff Broadhurst 2002

First published in 2002 by Easterhurst Publications Ltd
11, Warwick Close, Feniton, Devon, EX14 3DT.
Reprinted with revisions 2004

Printed and bound in England by
Short Run Press Ltd, Exeter, Devon.

Note:- The information given in this book has been provided in good faith and is intended for general guidance only. Whilst all reasonable efforts have been made to ensure that details were correct at the time of publication, the authors and publisher cannot accept responsibility for any inaccuracies which may result from changes that occur after going to print. It remains the responsibility of any person undertaking outdoor pursuits, to approach them with caution, and, if inexperienced, to do so under proper supervision. The walk described in this book is not particularly strenuous, but you should still ensure that you are fit enough to complete any section you embark upon.

The popularity of the first book and the re-opening of Section 10 of the walk, which had been closed due to a landslip between Gosford Bridge and Head Weir, has resulted in this reprinted version. We have taken the opportunity to include any changes that have occurred since the first printing and these appear on Page 56, replacing details of the temporary diversion (Section 10A). You should therefore check Page 56 for possible changes before commencing any section of the walk.

Cover Photographs
Front - The Otter Estuary
Back - Otterhead Lakes (Upper Lake)

PREFACE

After air and sunlight, water is mankind's most precious commodity. Its presence, be it in the form of ocean, lake, river or garden pond, seems to exert an unfailing magnetism and fascination to all those who venture near it. Devon is fortunate in having more than its fair share of water, with its two coastlines attracting a host of visitors every year. Inland numerous rivers rise, principally from the heights of Dartmoor, Exmoor or the Blackdown Hills, before finding their way to the sea. With few exceptions the rivers complete their journeys at one of Devon's eleven estuaries, more than in any other County in England.

Walking is undoubtedly one of the most popular outdoor leisure pursuits in this country, and, by using the vast network of public rights of way, a means of access to the countryside is available which enables it to be enjoyed by all. Over the years we have gained much pleasure and satisfaction from walking alongside Devon's rivers, whilst at the same time exploring the varied and delightful countryside through which they flow. The idea for this series of books, of which this is the second, originated as a result of us deciding to set out to walk as many of Devon's rivers as we could. There are many excellent books, guides and information packs on the subject of Devon's rivers, or parts of rivers, however we could find none that gave a 'walking boots' eye view of what is to be encountered when walking an entire river from source to sea. In this book every stile, gate and footbridge along the way is mentioned, in fact all that you pass by, go through, over, under or across, by walking the described route.

Through this series of books we wish to share with you the immense enjoyment, pleasure and sense of achievement that walking these rivers gave us, and hope that the books will encourage you to embark upon **WALKING DEVON'S RIVERS** yourself.

Richard Easterbrook
&
Geoff Broadhurst

Also available in the series entitled
'WALKING DEVON'S RIVERS'

THE RIVER AXE
ISBN 0 9538272 0 8

At the time of going to print the following books,
in the same series, were in the course of preparation

THE RIVER TEIGN
THE RIVER BOVEY and RIVER LEMON

ACKNOWLEDGEMENTS

This book was made possible with the help of many people. The Authors would like to extend their thanks to staff at Devon County Council's Environment Directorate for their assistance when we needed to check and verify the rights of way information. Thanks are also due to the staff at the County Library in Exeter for their patience and enthusiasm in helping us to obtain useful sources of information.

As with our previous book 'guinea pigs' either volunteered or were press-ganged into carrying out the unenviable task of walking the route using only the directions and sketches given in this book. Our grateful thanks therefore to Sharon Macey, Frances Easterbrook and Ian Yates all of whom, we are pleased to say, arrived at their intended destinations none the worst for their experiences! Thanks are again due to Wendy Lane for checking the text. To those who have also helped but we have not mentioned - thank you.

CONTENTS

PART 1
GENERAL ADVICE FOR WALKERS

EQUIPMENT, SAFETY and COMFORT

The walk generally involves either road or field walking and ranges from a few fairly steep sections to the more gentle rambles alongside the Otter itself. Although you will not need the same degree of preparation that is required for the rigours of moorland walking, it is still necessary to wear appropriate footwear and clothing. You should also carry a waterproof in case the weather changes. As there are only a few places along the way where you may be able to obtain food and drink, you should carry sufficient supplies with you depending upon the distance you intend to walk. We also recommend that you take the Ordnance Survey 'Explorer' Maps: 115 (Exmouth & Sidmouth), 116 (Lyme Regis & Bridport) and 128 (Taunton & Blackdown Hills) as these cover the whole walk and will assist you in identifying features along the route.

PUBLIC RIGHTS OF WAY

The Definitive Map

All Public Rights of Way are shown on a 'Definitive Map'. This is the legal record of the Public Rights of Way in each County. It was produced in England and Wales as a result of the 1949 National Parks & Access to the Countryside Act. Local Authorities are obliged to keep the maps up to date to show any legal changes to the network. Each Right of Way has a unique number according to the Parish it is in and what type of Right of Way it is, for example: Otterton - Footpath 3 or Upottery - Bridleway 25. Ordnance Survey 'Explorer', 'Landranger' and 'Outdoor Leisure' Maps show most public rights of way but will obviously not show any changes made after the maps were published. You should also note that not all footpaths and tracks etc shown on Ordnance Survey maps are public rights of way.

The Rights of Way used by the route described in this book were checked against the Definitive Maps of both Somerset and Devon in February 2002.

Types of Rights of Way

Three categories of Public Right of Way exist, which, along with their basic legal definitions, are as follows:-

Footpath (Yellow Waymark)
A highway over which the public have a right of way on foot only.

Bridleway (Blue Waymark)
A highway over which the public have a right of way on foot, or to ride or lead a horse (or mule or donkey). Pedal cycles are also allowed but cyclists have to give way to pedestrians and riders. There is no right to drive a vehicle.

Byway (Red Waymark)

A highway over which the public not only have a right of way as for bridleways, but for vehicular use as well.

A further right of way known as a **'Permissive Path'** (Green Waymark) also exists, but the right of passage is at the discretion of the landowner and can be withdrawn at any time.

The Use of Public Rights of Way

A Right of Way is what it implies - it is a right of passage over the ground. You do not have the right to roam at will or use the ground for any other purpose. Whilst Right of Ways should be kept open and unobstructed you should bear in mind that landowners are not obliged to provide a good surface or signpost the route across their land. Although you are required to keep to the correct line at all times, this is not always possible, or is sometimes impractical to do so. For example, you may come across a fallen tree or branch, or a deliberate illegal obstruction such as a barbed wire fence. In either case, you are allowed to remove the obstacle sufficiently to get past or you may take a short alternative route around it. You are also permitted to take a short detour, (keeping close to a field boundary wherever possible) to overcome a broken stile or footbridge for example.

THE COUNTRY CODE

Remember that by following the Country Code and using the paths properly, you are much less likely to encounter problems.

- Enjoy the countryside and respect its life and work.
- Guard against all risk of fire
- Fasten all gates
- Keep your dogs under close control, and always on a lead when there is livestock around
- Keep to the public paths
- Use gates and stiles to cross fences, hedges and walls
- Leave livestock, crops and machinery alone
- Take your litter home
- Help to keep all water clean
- Take special care on country roads - face oncoming traffic
- Protect wildlife, plants and trees

AND MOST IMPORTANT OF ALL

- **TAKE NOTHING**   -   but photographs and memories
- **LEAVE NOTHING**   -   but footprints

PART 2
THE ROUTE

THE COURSE OF THE RIVER OTTER

Total length	28 miles
Source	Nr Yalham Farm at Grid Reference ST 218151
Finish	Otterton Ledge at Grid Reference SY 078819
Height at Source	251 metres (825 feet)
Main Tributaries	'Luppit Stream', Rivers Wolf and Tale

The Otter is one of only a few of Devon's rivers that have their source outside the County. Although the river begins its journey in the **Blackdown Hills** in Somerset, a short distance to the west of **Yalham Farm,** only the first few miles of it are in that county before it crosses into Devon. Rising at a height of some 825 feet (251m) above sea level the Otter starts its journey in a southerly direction, passing to the west of the small hamlet of **Otterford,** before forming the two man-made lakes called **Otterhead Lakes.** Shortly after these lakes and **Royston Water** the Otter quietly enters Devon at Fry's Moor, to the south-east of the village of **Churchinford.** Continuing its journey southwards as far as 'Charleshayes Farmhouse' the river then takes a south-westerly course towards the small village of **Upottery,** which it passes to the south-east. After passing to the north-west of the hamlet of **Rawridge** the Otter continues on a south-westerly route flowing below the eastern slopes of **Dumpdon Hill,** a prehistoric hillfort. Still on a south-westerly course the river then makes its way towards the market town of **Honiton,** which it skirts to the north. Honiton is famous for its lace and pottery and has a long straight main street along the line of an old Roman road. Directly to the north of Honiton, and on the other side of the Otter, the village of **Combe Raleigh** nestles on the hillside. After taking a slightly more westerly course through the hamlet of **Weston** and then on towards **Buckerell,** passed to the south, the river flows through **Fenny Meadows,** the site of an historic battle fought in 1549. After flowing under the A30 road bridge to the north-east of **Fenny Bridges,** the river then flows under two fine brick arch structures carrying the railway and the B3177 road, before reaching the small hamlet of **Alfington**. Within a couple of miles the town of **Ottery St Mary,** famous for its flaming tar barrels ceremony, is reached after which the river takes the southerly course which it maintains for the remainder of its journey. The small village of **Tipton St John** is passed within a few miles and after a further mile and a half the river passes between the small village of **Harpford** and the much larger village of **Newton Poppleford.** Two more villages, **Colaton Raleigh** to the west and then **Otterton** to the east, are passed before the Otter enters its tidal reaches to the east of **East Budleigh.** Only now, as the river nears journey's end, do the seemingly never ending open fields give way to a vertical cliff face on the eastern side of its estuary. The river finally squeezes between the cliffs and a high pebble ridge which over the years has contrived to block the Otter's more direct route to the sea. The red sandstone cliffs to the east of the town of **Budleigh Salterton** form a magnificent backdrop as it enters the sea at the end of it's twenty eight mile journey.

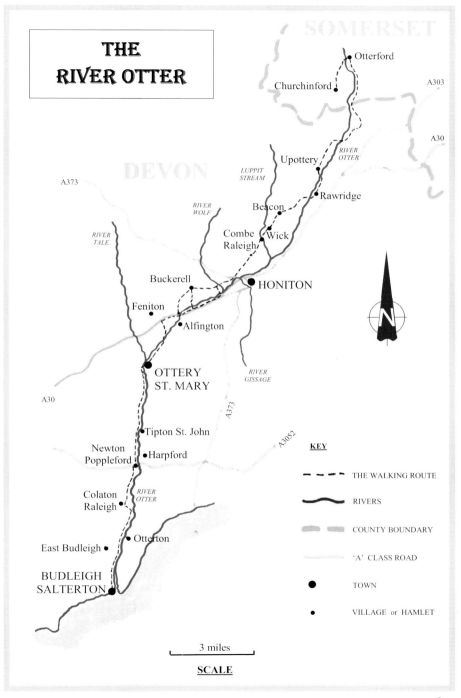

THE RIVER OTTER

SOMERSET

Otterford

Churchinford

A303

A30

DEVON

A373

RIVER OTTER

Upottery

LUPPIT STREAM

Rawridge

RIVER WOLF

Beacon

RIVER TALE

Combe Raleigh

Wick

Buckerell

HONITON

Feniton

Alfington

OTTERY ST. MARY

RIVER GISSAGE

A30

A373

Tipton St. John

Newton Poppleford

Harpford

A3052

KEY

Colaton Raleigh

RIVER OTTER

Otterton

East Budleigh

BUDLEIGH SALTERTON

- - - - THE WALKING ROUTE

~~~~ RIVERS

COUNTY BOUNDARY

'A' CLASS ROAD

● TOWN

• VILLAGE or HAMLET

N

3 miles

SCALE

PART 3
THE WALK

WALK DETAILS

Total length	32.16 miles (max) 30.96 miles (min)
Start	Churchinford at Grid Reference ST 213126
Finish	Budleigh Salterton at Grid Reference SY 077819
Highest point reached	Dumpdon Hill at 261 metres (856 feet)
Towns, Villages and	Churchinford, Upottery, Beacon, Wick, Combe Raleigh,
Hamlets along the route	(Honiton), Weston, Buckerell, Ottery St Mary,
	Tipton St John, Newton Poppleford, Colaton Raleigh,
	Otterton, and Budleigh Salterton.

The Otter is one of the most tranquil rivers that shape Devon's beautiful landscape. Although it rises in Somerset, high in the Blackdown Hills, only the first couple of miles of its journey are in that County. After these initial stages the Otter then flows entirely within the south-eastern corner of Devon for the remaining twenty six miles of its journey. Flowing through the lush green countryside that characterises this part of the County, the occasional weir only serves to momentarily interrupt its sure but gentle progress to the sea. Some sources suggest that the river got its name long before Saxon times. The Anglo-Saxon for the name of the animal was 'ōter' to which was added 'ēā' meaning water or stream thus combining as 'Ōterēā' or 'Otter River'. Others suggest it simply acquired its name from the animal itself and, after a steady decline, Otters are now showing welcome signs of an increase in numbers.

WALK DESCRIPTIONS

The walk as described in this book is just over thirty two miles long. It has been designed as a continuous walk over two or three days but can be done in smaller sections or over a longer period of time. The descriptions and accompanying sketch maps which have been produced are based on a route which has been walked by us many times. We hope that the book will be of use to everyone who enjoys walking and that the descriptions and sketch maps present an easy to follow guide.

However, the passage of time can introduce changes at the hands of both man and nature; that signpost or stile may no longer be there, or that footbridge washed away. There is also the distinct possibility that a footpath may have become re-routed or even new ones introduced. For example, where landslips have occurred or if changes in farming methods have to be accommodated. Most landowners tend to be very co-operative in keeping rights of way clear, indeed whilst walking this particular route we did not come across any blatant obstructions of any kind.

The English seasons do of course present their own natural challenges to the walker, from the sometimes overgrown grass, nettles and brambles of summer, to the boggy and slippery surfaces in winter. Such seasonal problems are easily overcome by those wearing suitable gear. Although the Otter is not particularly prone to large scale flooding, care should be taken after prolonged periods of rain as this will inevitably result in very wet ground, making some field sections of the walk extremely difficult in places. Apart from a diversion near Ottery St Mary which may be necessary due to landslips on the preferred route, we have not attempted to suggest possible alternatives in this book. Any experienced walker armed with the relevant Ordnance Survey map should have no difficulty in finding an alternative route should the need arise.

As far as possible, the walk has been deliberately routed to use only footpaths, bridleways and byways, but some road walking is inevitable. The 'Nature Trail' through the Otterhead Lakes area is a permissive path which, although unlikely, could be closed at any time. The maps and descriptions, when read in conjunction with an Ordnance Survey Map, should make it possible for you to complete the walk without any problems. With a few exceptions, the route of the walk is reasonably well signposted and waymarked on the ground, but may not always be straightforward to follow without the aid of this book and a map.

PLANNING YOUR WALK

General

For those of you who wish to complete the walk with the minimal amount of stops, we would suggest that you make it a two day walk; from Churchinford to Honiton on the first day, and then the remainder to Budleigh Salterton on the second day. If however, you wish to spend time looking around the various places of interest along the way, we would suggest that you split the walk into three days, covering Churchinford to Upottery, Upottery to Ottery St Mary, and finally the remainder to Budleigh Salterton. It should be possible for you to cover each of these lengths in a day, to include refreshment stops etc, and still have ample time to look around. In either of the above cases, and with the lone walker in mind, we have taken into consideration the availability of car parking and public transport along the way. This ensures that no retracing of steps should be necessary to get back again. Our own preference was to leave a car at a convenient 'finish' point and then use public transport to get to the 'start'. There are two advantages in doing this; firstly, it acts as a good safeguard should the 'unexpected' happen, such as no bus turning up at the far end; secondly, it gives you the opportunity to walk without having to keep an 'eye on the clock'.

Accommodation

In **Part 4** we have included a list of accommodation addresses which is not intended to be comprehensive or to be a recommendation of any individual property. It is merely a selection of those we have noticed along or near the route. Towns such as Honiton, Ottery St Mary and Budleigh Salterton have numerous accommodation possibilities and therefore we have not attempted to list them all. Any of the local Tourist Information Centres, also listed in **Part 4,** will be able to help you find suitable accommodation in these towns and the surrounding areas.

USING THE SKETCHES
AND WALK DESCRIPTIONS

General

The whole walk from Churchinford to Budleigh Salterton has been divided into seventeen sections. These have largely been determined by the need to clearly define the route using what we hope are concise, easy to follow notes and sketch maps. As a result each section on average covers just under two miles. The actual length of a section is indicated at the head of the page immediately opposite the corresponding sketch map.

Places of Interest and Facilities

Brief descriptive notes on places and points of interest along the way have been included wherever possible. Facilities available on or near the route have also been indicated, either in the notes themselves, or on the sketch maps. To assist you in planning ahead, particularly when walking in the more remote sections, we have indicated distances to the next available facilities.

Transport

Bus Stops and Service Numbers have been marked on the maps and afford the opportunity to break your journey if necessary. Because bus services and times are liable to frequent changes, only the current services and their operators have been listed in **Part 4,** along with Train and Taxi operators.

SYMBOLS USED

A ◉ symbol in the text description indicates the start of paragraphs containing the actual walking directions, which are **highlighted in bold.**

Key to Sketch Map Symbols

FP	Footpath	FB	Footbridge
BW	Bridleway	Wk	Waymark
WC	Public Convenience	PO	Post Office
G	Garage (selling refreshments etc)	LC	Level Crossing
S	Shop (in villages only)	PH	Public House
TIC	Tourist Information Centre	GP	Guide Post
•—•	Gate or Stile	—	Wall (brick, stone or concrete)
] [	Bridge	ⅢⅢ	Fence (wood, iron or wire)
■■■	Railway	aaaa	Hedge or Scrub
(	Public Telephone	⌐⌐	Panoramic View

➡ **Start of Section** — — — — **The Walking Route**

12

THE START OF YOUR WALK

The immediate area around Otterford in which the Otter rises is not served directly by public transport and as a result it is only possible to get to it either on foot or by car. We have therefore started the walk at Churchinford which is about a mile and a half to the south of the Otter's source. You can then walk to Otterford and down through the Otterhead Lakes Nature Reserve to Royston Water. From there you can either continue on along the main walking route or return to Churchinford without having to retrace your steps. There are two further opportunities to return to Churchinford in Section 3 of the walk.

Note:- Before setting off from Churchinford you should bear in mind that unless you time your walk to arrive at Upottery (just over 7½ miles) when the pub (The Sidmouth Arms) is open, there is no other opportunity for refreshments in the first 15 miles or so of the walk, and even then you will need to visit Honiton.

Churchinford

Churchinford, with its star shaped layout, stands at the meeting place of several roads, the most important of which runs from Taunton to Honiton. By being at the crossing point of two Roman roads, branches of the Fosse Way and the Icknield Way, it is possible that in Roman times a settlement existed here. Churchinford's church is not in the village but is unusually situated over a mile and a half to the north-west at Churchstanton which conversely has no village. The name Churchinford is thought to have derived from the chapel-of-ease (church-en-ford) that used to exist near Fairhouse Farm to the west of the ford over the Otter. The remains of the chapel are now barely discernable. The village itself contains a number of 15th and 16th century cottages. Part of the York Inn also dates from this time and some time ago, when

Churchinford

the roof was being repaired, a priest's chamber was discovered along with a sword of the Commonwealth period. A similar Cromwellian sword was found during repairs to the nearby post office. For those of you with an interest in gems of useless knowledge, it was a former resident of Churchinford, a Miss Violet Wellesley who, when a junior commander of a training unit at Windsor in World War II, taught our present Queen Elizabeth to drive!

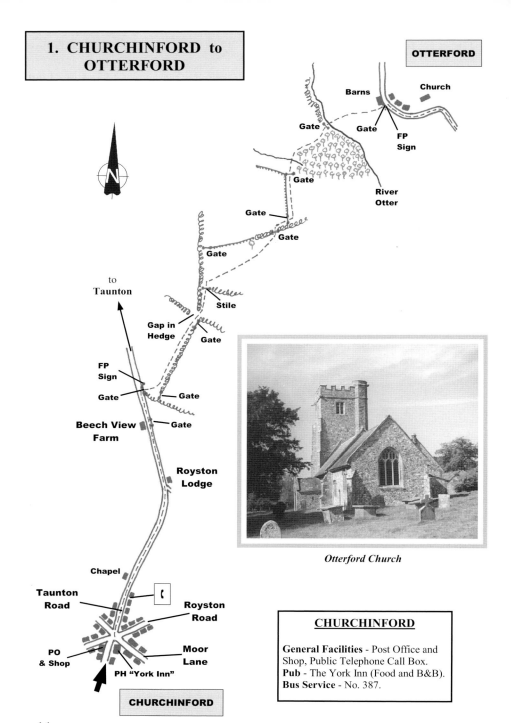

1. CHURCHINFORD to OTTERFORD

OTTERFORD

Barns

Church

Gate

Gate

FP
Sign

Gate

River
Otter

Gate

Gate

Gate

to
Taunton

Stile

Gap in
Hedge

Gate

FP
Sign

Gate

Gate

Beech View
Farm

Gate

Royston
Lodge

Chapel

Taunton
Road

Royston
Road

PO
& Shop

Moor
Lane

PH "York Inn"

CHURCHINFORD

Otterford Church

CHURCHINFORD

General Facilities - Post Office and
Shop, Public Telephone Call Box.
Pub - The York Inn (Food and B&B).
Bus Service - No. 387.

⊘ **From the centre of Churchinford take the road signed as 'Taunton Road', and follow this uphill for about a quarter of a mile** passing first a small chapel on the left and then, a little further on, 'Royston Lodge' on the right. **About fifty yards after passing 'Beech View Farm'** on your left (the farm's name may not be displayed) **you come to a metal gate and footpath sign** on the right. **Go through the gate into a field and aim for the hedge in front of you. At the hedge bear left and continue by keeping close to the right-hand edge of the field until you see two gaps in the hedge in front of you** and a gate in the hedge on your right. **Go through the right-hand gap and** keeping the hedge on your left **go down to a stile. Go over the stile and into the next field**. The next field boundary down in front of you is formed of a fence which joins a hedge about a third of the way along. **Head diagonally right to a metal gate** which you will see in the hedge section of this boundary. **Go through the gate and turn right. Follow the hedge to a metal gate** in the post and wire fence ahead of you. **Go through the gate and immediately turn left. Keeping the post and wire fence on your left, go downhill to another metal gate** alongside a wood. **Go through the gate and** keep close to the right-hand field boundary **down to a stream. Cross over the stream and** keeping the wood on your right **continue on to a metal field gate. Go through the gate** and there immediately in front of you is your first glimpse of the Otter. The actual source of the Otter is about half a mile further upstream. **Step over the water and then aim for the right-hand side of the farm buildings** up in front of you. **Go around the side of a barn**, which has a 'footpath' direction sign on it, **to a metal gate. Go through the gate and out onto the road.** If you turn left the source of the Otter is about half a mile up the road. **For the walk turn right past 'Church Farm',** formally a mill known to date back to at least the late 13th century, **and then follow the road round to the left until you arrive at Otterford Church.**

Otterford

The buildings which make up Otterford consist only of the Church of St Leonard, which is mainly 19th century, the nearby 'Church Farm', a few cottages and the Lodge at the entrance to the Otterhead Estate. The Parish Church can claim to have one of the most spacious graveyards in Somerset with even room set aside for a public footpath that runs diagonally through it.

Otterford viewed from 'The Lodge'

Inside the Church there is a tablet erected in memory of William Beadon who died in 1864 and who built the nearby Otterhead Lakes and Estate which you will walk through in the next section of this walk.

15

2. OTTERFORD to ROYSTON WATER

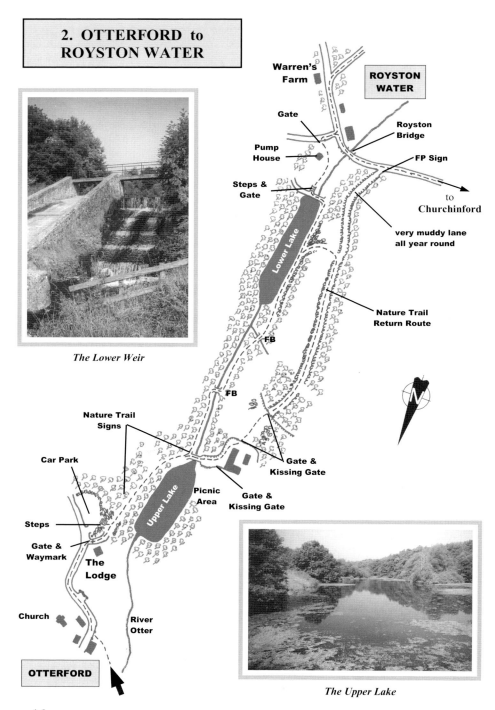

The Lower Weir

Warren's Farm

ROYSTON WATER

Gate

Royston Bridge

Pump House

FP Sign

Steps & Gate

to Churchinford

very muddy lane all year round

Lower Lake

Nature Trail Return Route

FB

FB

N

Nature Trail Signs

Car Park

Gate & Kissing Gate

Upper Lake

Picnic Area

Gate & Kissing Gate

Steps

Gate & Waymark

The Lodge

Church

River Otter

OTTERFORD

The Upper Lake

From the Church continue along the road and follow it round to the right and then on up to 'The Lodge' on your right. It is likely that the Head Gardener of the Otterhead Estate would have resided here. **Go through the single bar gate on the right** marked "Public Footpath" and "No cars beyond this point" **and follow the track downhill through the woods. You will eventually come to a bridge** with the 'Upper Lake' over to your right. The site of 'Otterhead House' and its terraced gardens was over on the far bank where picnic tables are now conveniently placed.

Otterhead Estate and Lakes

The lakes are situated in the grounds of the former Otterhead Estate and are now owned by the Wessex Water Authority. 'Otterhead House', which was built around 1841 by William Beadon, a Taunton surgeon, was demolished in 1952 with only the original stable blocks, used by the Red Cross during World War II, still remaining. Originally there were five lakes each connected by a system of leats, weirs and pumps. Now only two survive with water from the lower lake, known as 'Royston Water', being pumped over the Blackdown Hills to reservoirs which supply Taunton with its drinking water. Now a designated nature reserve, visitors are welcome to picnic and explore this peaceful and unspoilt area using the signed 'Nature Trail'. Marshy areas of the reserve can be treacherous so you are advised to keep to the marked trail.

The Lower Lake (Royston Water)

To continue the walk do not go across the bridge but instead **go down onto the path to the left** which is just before the bridge. This path is signed as a 'Nature Trail'. **Follow this path alongside the Otter,** still merely a stream in size, **and continue on to a footbridge which takes you to the other side.** The marshy surroundings you are now walking through was once the bottom of one of the original five lakes so do not stray from the path. **Continue on, crossing another footbridge, until you come to the side of the lower lake. Follow the edge of this lake as far as some wooden fencing** where the nature trail is signed off to the right and up away from the water's edge. **However you continue straight on alongside the lake. At the end of the lake go over the weir and then turn right down some steps, to a small wooden gate. Go through the gate and then, just past the pump house, bear left towards a small wooden gate,** almost hidden under the trees, to the left of a metal field gate. The other field gate, nearest to the river, is usually padlocked. **Go through the small gate and out onto the road turning right to go down to a junction.** If you wish to return to Churchinford turn right at the junction and the village is then about ¾ mile further along the road. **For the walk turn left and then after a short sharp climb, turn right** at the triangular shaped junction opposite 'Warren's Farm'.

17

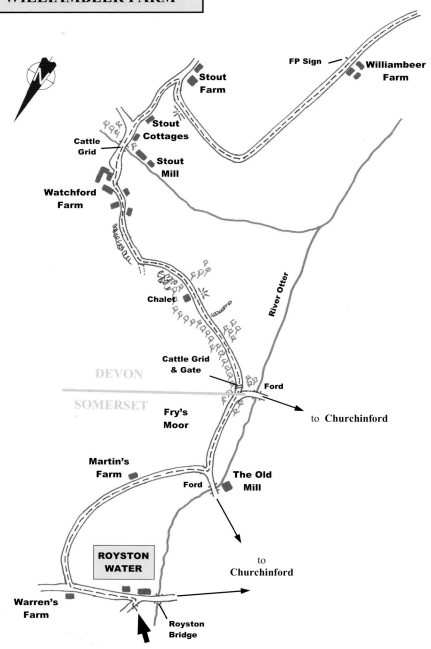

FP Sign

Williambeer Farm

Stout Farm

Stout Cottages

Cattle Grid

Stout Mill

Watchford Farm

River Otter

Chalet

Cattle Grid & Gate

Ford

DEVON

SOMERSET

Fry's Moor

to Churchinford

Martin's Farm

Ford

The Old Mill

ROYSTON WATER

to Churchinford

Warren's Farm

Royston Bridge

18

Continue along the road until it drops down to meet the River Otter again at Fry's Moor. At this point you can return to Churchinford by crossing the river and then continuing up along the lane for about ¾ mile. 'The Old Mill' across the river was known as 'Otriford Mill' in 1367 and ceased operating in 1906. **For the walk** do not cross the river but **bear left, and then continue along the road until it meets the river once more.** Again, by crossing the river, you can return to Churchinford. **For the walk take the unfenced road off to the left and go over a cattle grid.** You are now in Devon. **Go along the unfenced road** until at one point you can be forgiven for thinking you are in Switzerland as you go past a recently built 'Swiss Chalet' style building. From here there is a superb view down the Otter Valley. **After passing this chalet continue on along the road and down to 'Watchford Farm'. Bear right by the**

The Otter Valley near Watchford Farm

farm to go over a cattle grid and then a bridge over a small tributary stream of the Otter that feeds the nearby Stout Mill, **and then climb the steep hill past 'Stout Mill Cottage' and 'Stout Cottages'. Just before 'Stout Farm' turn right into a road** that offers fine views back over to the other side of the valley which you have just walked along. **Follow this road all the way to 'Williambeer Farm'.**

The Blackdown Hills

This book would not be complete without a few words about the area you have been walking through since leaving Churchinford. The Blackdown Hills are a group of hills lying on the boundary between Somerset and Devon and were designated as an Area of Outstanding Natural Beauty in June 1991. The total area of about 370 sq km can be very broadly defined as extending from Wellington in the north to Honiton in the south and from Cullompton in the west to Chard in the east. The north side consists of a steep wooded escarpment whereas in complete contrast the southern side slopes away gently, broken only by river valleys. Along these valleys, set in their pastoral surroundings, nestle numerous villages, hamlets and farms all connected by quiet country lanes similar to the ones you follow on parts of this walk. The whole area is sparsely populated and is totally devoid of any towns, with the unspoilt landscape retaining many traditional methods of farming which further serve to enhance the relative peace and tranquillity of the area. It also contains sites of historical importance such as Hembury Fort. Today the Blackdowns are managed by a rural partnership whose aim is to ensure that the area will lose none of its unique charm. Of the three main 'Devon' rivers that rise in the Blackdowns only the Otter eventually flows into its own estuary at the end of its journey. The other two, the Culm and the Yarty are tributaries of the rivers Exe and Axe respectively.

4. WILLIAMBEER FARM to UPOTTERY

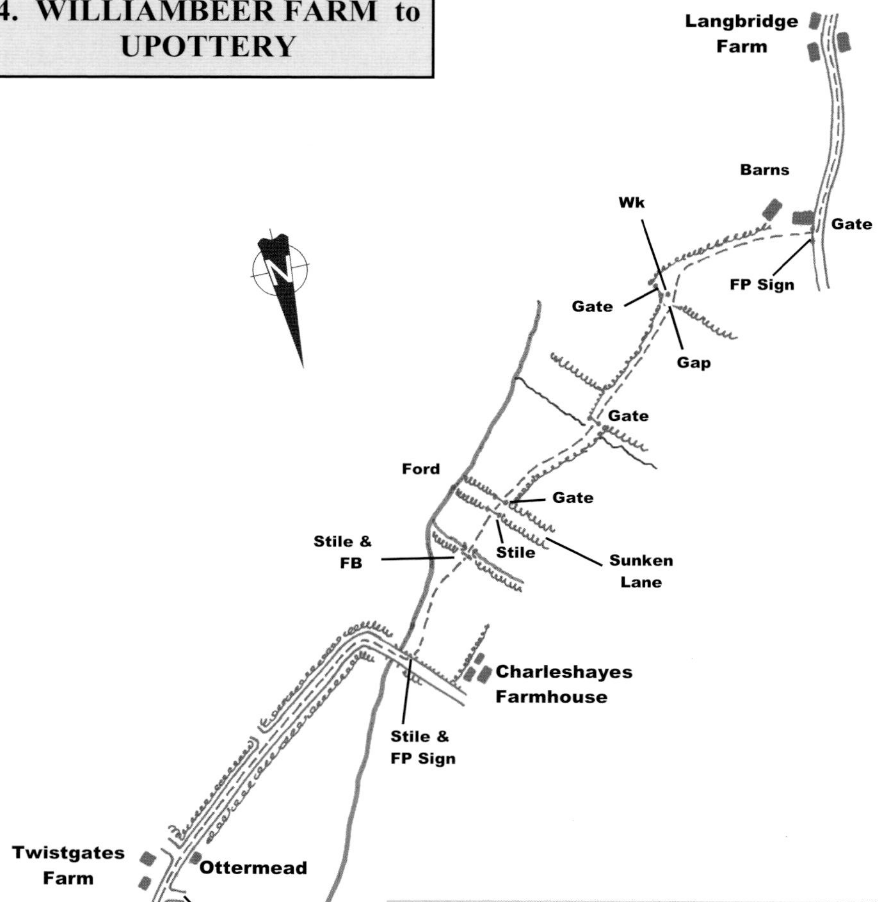

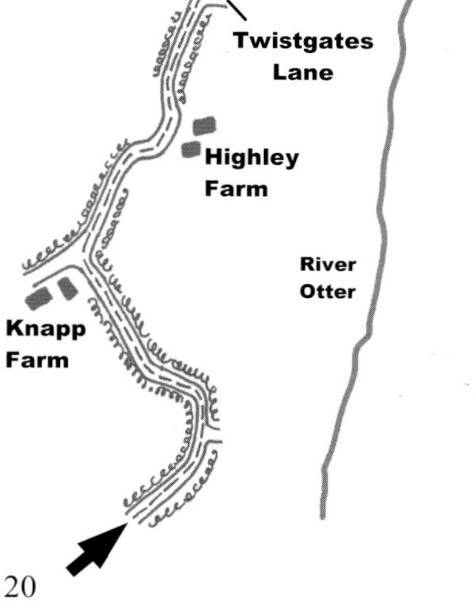

Langbridge Farm

Barns

Wk

Gate

Gate

FP Sign

Gap

Gate

Ford

Gate

Stile & FB

Stile

Sunken Lane

Charleshayes Farmhouse

Stile & FP Sign

Twistgates Farm

Ottermead

Twistgates Lane

Highley Farm

River Otter

Knapp Farm

The Otter downstream from Charleshayes Farmhouse

From 'Williambeer Farm' continue along the road for some distance until eventually, just past a road on your right which goes down to the river, it climbs steadily up to 'Knapp Farm' and a road junction. Here turn right and go past 'Highley Farm'. Continue along the road, ignoring Twistgates Lane (unsigned) to your right, until you get to 'Ottermead' also on your right. Here go straight ahead along the lane and continue on until eventually it goes round to the right towards a bridge. Immediately after crossing the Otter there is a stile and footpath sign in the left-hand fence. Cross the stile and then go across the field keeping the river alongside you on your left. When the river turns away to the left, carry on straight across the field to a stile. Go over the stile and a plank footbridge into the next field. Go straight across the field to another stile. Cross the stile which leads into a sunken lane and go straight across the lane to a metal gate on the other side. Go through the gate into a field. Keeping the hedge on your right follow it to another gate just beyond a stream. Go through the gate and turn left to go uphill keeping a fence and then a hedge on your left. Continue on to a waymark post by a gap in the hedge at the end of the field. Continue through the next field keeping the hedge on your left, past an old farm shed and barn, to a metal gate which leads out onto a road. Turn left and follow this road, which is usually very muddy, past 'Langbridge Farm' to a road junction. At the junction bear right and go along the road, passing Upottery's village hall on your right, until you reach a war memorial at a road junction. If you require refreshments the 'Sidmouth Arms' is immediately on your right. The row of thatched cottages on your left was where the local village fire brigade kept its own hand pump until the early 1950's.

Upottery

Upottery is the first village in Devon on the Otter, lying in pleasant pastoral surroundings sheltered by hills on either side of the valley. It is believed to have origins dating back to Saxon times. The Manor was bought by Dr John Addington in 1759 and his son Henry, the first Viscount Sidmouth, was Prime Minister from 1801 to 1804. The 'Sidmouth Arms' public house is named after him. At the time of the Norman Conquest the Church of St Mary was in the possession of Rouen Cathedral but was taken over by

The Sidmouth Arms and St Mary's Church

Exeter Cathedral in 1267. It has a Norman tower and was restored in 1875. The vicar of Upottery from 1886 to 1923 was the Rev. John Jane whose son Frederick was the author of 'Jane's All the World's Fighting Ships' to which he later added a similar book on aircraft. Today these constantly updated works are globally regarded as the ultimate reference source for defence, aerospace and transportation information.

5. UPOTTERY to MOHUN'S OTTERY

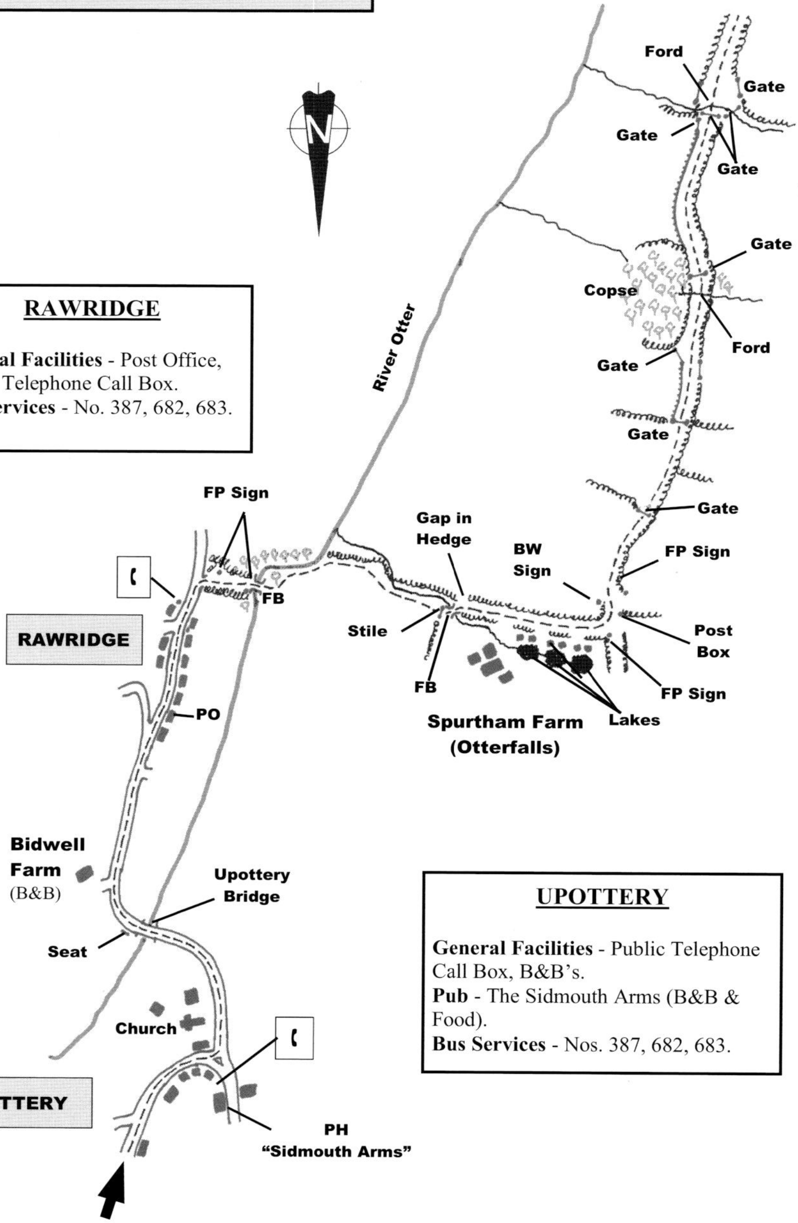

Ford

Gate

Gate

Gate

Gate

Copse

Ford

Gate

Gate

Gate

River Otter

RAWRIDGE

General Facilities - Post Office, Public Telephone Call Box.
Bus Services - No. 387, 682, 683.

FP Sign

Gap in Hedge

BW Sign

FP Sign

FB

RAWRIDGE

Stile

Post Box

FB

FP Sign

PO

Spurtham Farm (Otterfalls)

Lakes

Bidwell Farm
(B&B)

Upottery Bridge

Seat

UPOTTERY

General Facilities - Public Telephone Call Box, B&B's.
Pub - The Sidmouth Arms (B&B & Food).
Bus Services - Nos. 387, 682, 683.

Church

UPOTTERY

PH
"Sidmouth Arms"

⬛ **At the memorial turn left and go down the road, past the church, to the bridge over the Otter.** From here you get a splendid view back to the old vicarage built in 1843. **After the bridge,** and a conveniently situated seat if you need a rest, **the road bears right** past Bidwell Farm **and then continues on to Rawridge.**

Rawridge

Rawridge is mentioned in the Domesday Book as Rouerige owned by St Mary's Church, Rouen in France who also owned Ottery St Mary. At one time Rawridge had its own Church, Manor House and an annual fair. The Church did not survive beyond the Reformation and was bought by Sir John Popham around 1600. Most of the stone from the church was lost to road building although some of the beams, a pointed stone arch window and a doorway from the original church can still be seen at 'Chapelhouse' in the village.

⬛ **Bear right at a Y junction and continue on through Rawridge. About eighty yards after 'Otter Vale Close'** on the left, **you will come to a lane** on your right. **Turn right into the lane** (note:- the footpath sign is a few yards down the lane, on the left-hand side, not near the edge of the road itself) **and go down to a footbridge** across the Otter. **Cross over and then go left alongside the river for a short distance before heading off right to go up the field** alongside the field boundary and a small stream **to a stile. Cross the stile and bear left over the stream and then continue on up a lane past 'Spurtham Farm'** now a leisure facility called 'Otterfalls'. **Continue up the lane** past the chalets and lakes, (these are on private

Footbridge near Rawridge

land), **until it joins another lane at the top. Here turn left onto a bridleway which goes into the field immediately on your left** (not the more obvious track which bears off to the right). **Keeping the hedge on your right follow the field edge to a gate. Go through this and continue,** keeping the hedge on your right, **to another gate** which leads on to a roughly surfaced track. **Go along this track passing through two more gates and crossing three small fords until you reach 'Mohun's Ottery'** on your left.

Mohun's Ottery was built in the 13th century by Sir Reginald Mohun. In 1280 it became the home of the Carew family, descendents of whom have since played a major role in Devon's history. Originally from South Wales the family came to Devon during the reign of Edward I. In 1549 Sir Peter Carew helped Lord Russell's forces overthrow an uprising by Devonshire and Cornish rebels at Fenny Meadows (which you can visit in Section 9 of the walk). Sir George Carew went down with the 'Mary Rose'. The property was rebuilt in 1868 after a fire, but the remains of a 16th century gatehouse are still there.

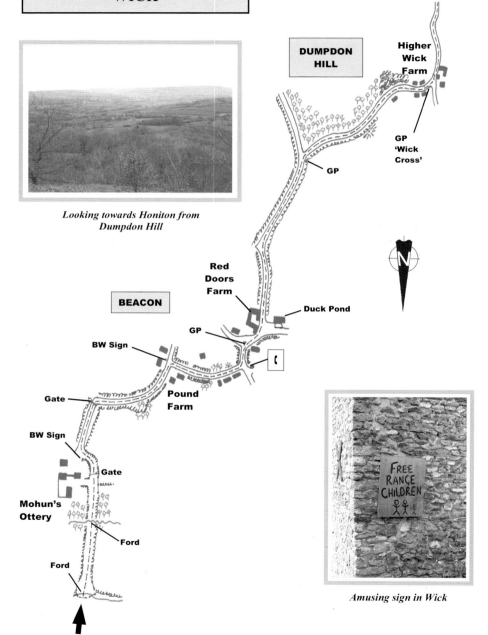

Looking towards Honiton from Dumpdon Hill

DUMPDON HILL

Higher Wick Farm

GP 'Wick Cross'

GP

Red Doors Farm

BEACON

Duck Pond

GP

BW Sign

Pound Farm

Gate

BW Sign

Gate

Mohun's Ottery

Ford

Ford

FREE RANGE CHILDREN

Amusing sign in Wick

⬤ **After passing 'Mohun's Ottery' continue on the track until it bears slightly left to a surfaced road.** If you look back to your left into the grounds of 'Mohun's Ottery' you can see the remains of an arched doorway. **Turn right onto the surfaced road. Go along the road until it bends right and continue on to 'Pound Farm',** which was built in the late 17th century. **Here turn right and go up the steep hill to Beacon passing some delightful cottages** with superb views out over the Otter valley towards Honiton. Beacon nestles into the side of the slope at the southern end of the hillfort of Hartridge. **At the next road junction turn left down the hill and where the road forks, bear right** (signposted 'Luppit') **and then immediately left down past 'Red Doors Farm',** a five hundred year old thatched farmhouse. **Continue along the road which steadily climbs towards Dumpdon Hill. As you approach the hillfort you will come to a road signposted right to Wick.** If you wish to go to the top of Dumpdon Hill do not turn

Beacon

right but carry straight on up the road until you come to a car park on the right. From the car park you can then walk to the top of the hillfort.

Dumpdon Hill

Crowned by a group of beech trees this pear-shaped Iron Age hillfort is a prominent landscape feature, lying to the north-east of Honiton. It provides superb views in all directions, particularly of the Otter valley, and it is well worth the short steep deviation away from the walking route to the summit at 856 feet (261m). Although not too obvious when viewed at ground level, there are two substantial ramparts on the northern side (being the side which was most vulnerable to enemy attack) and smaller single ramparts to the east and west. Extending to an area of just over six acres, the hillfort is now owned by the National Trust.

⬤ **For the walk turn right onto the road** signposted to Wick. If you now look back towards Beacon the hillfort of Hartridge dominates the skyline. **Follow this road** which skirts round the northern edge of Dumpdon Hill, **all the way towards Wick** keeping an eye out for the amusing sign "free range children" on the side of the farm building to your right. **At 'Wick Cross' turn left and continue down to the hamlet of Wick itself.**

25

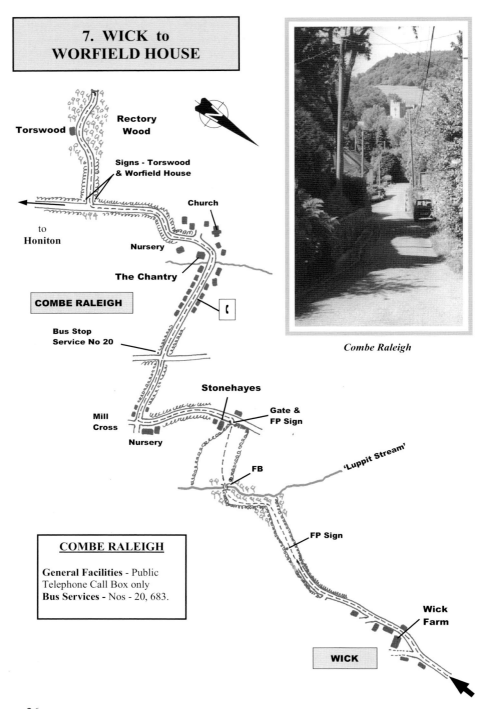

7. WICK to WORFIELD HOUSE

Torswood

Rectory Wood

Signs - Torswood & Worfield House

to Honiton

Church

Nursery

The Chantry

COMBE RALEIGH

Bus Stop Service No 20

Stonehayes

Mill Cross

Gate & FP Sign

Nursery

FB

'Luppit Stream'

COMBE RALEIGH

General Facilities - Public Telephone Call Box only
Bus Services - Nos - 20, 683.

FP Sign

Wick Farm

WICK

Combe Raleigh

⬤ Go down through the hamlet of Wick and continue on until the metalled road becomes a roughly surfaced lane. Carry on down this lane, passing a footpath sign on your left, **until you near a stream** (known locally as the 'Luppit Stream'). **As you approach the stream bear left into a copse and continue on through the copse to a footbridge. Cross over the footbridge into the field and then head diagonally up the field towards the metal gate** to the right of the farm buildings. **Go through the gate and onto the road and turn left** passing 'Stonehayes'. **Continue on along this road until you reach the nursery at 'Mill Cross'. Here turn right and go uphill until you eventually come to the junction with the main** Honiton to Dunkeswell **road. Go straight across this road and down through the village of Combe Raleigh.**

Combe Raleigh

Known as Combawton in Henry III's time the village has since had several changes of name before becoming what it is known as today. Combe Raleigh is a neat little village with several old cottages and buildings of note among which is 'Chantry House', a late 15th century priest's house which is thought to be connected with a chantry founded here in 1498. The Abbot's House was built in 1790 and was used as a prisoner of war camp in World War II. The village was owned by the Raleigh family in the 13th century. Several prehistoric burial mounds have been found to the north of the village. The Church of St Nicholas is a 15th century building.

St Nicholas Church, Combe Raleigh

⬤ About a quarter of a mile after leaving the village you arrive at a turning on the right signposted 'Torswood' and 'Worfield House'. Unless you wish to go to Honiton (see notes below) **turn right here and go uphill past 'Torswood' continuing along the lane** through woods **until you come to the gate of Worfield House.**

Note:- If you wish to go to Honiton do not turn right to 'Torswood' and 'Worfield House' but instead continue on along the road straight ahead and Honiton is about ¾ mile away. You can also continue with the next section of the walk when a further opportunity to visit Honiton arises.

27

Honiton

Early Closing - *Thursday (but many shops remain open).* **Cattle Market** - *Tuesday,* **Street Market** - *Tuesday and Saturday.* **General Facilities** - *Post Office, Banks, Hotels and B&B's, Shops, Restaurants, Cafes, Library and other such facilities expected to be found in a market town of this size.* **Pubs** - *The following are all in the town centre and all do food:- Vine Inn, Volunteer, Three Tuns, White Lion (B&B), Red Cow, Carlton, Star, Railway Inn, New Dolphin (B&B), Honiton Wine Bar. On the western outskirts of the town are:- The Honiton Motel and The Heathfield both of which do food and B&B.* **Bus Services** - *Nos.20, 340, 379, 380, 387, 682, 683, 694.* **Railway Station** - *Services to London (Waterloo) and Exeter.* **Tourist Information Centre** - *in Lace Walk car park.* **Museum** - *Allhallows Museum, High Street, contains a world class collection of lace as well as exhibitions and demonstrations of lace-making. Open: 10.00pm to 5.00pm Monday to Saturday from the Monday before Easter to the end of October (closes 4.00pm in October) Tel: 01404 44966*

Market Day in Honiton's High Street

Honiton is an ancient borough and market town and is often referred to as the gateway to Devon. Picturesquely situated on rising ground, on the southern side of the river Otter, the name is derived from the Saxon 'Huna's Tun' (farm belonging to Huna). Although served from the east by the busy A30, A303 and A35 trunk roads, Honiton is only linked to many surrounding picturesque villages such as Dalwood, Combe Raleigh, Upottery and Gittisham by means of narrow winding country roads.

Honiton, which is twinned with Mezidon-Canon in France and Gronau in Germany, is still traditionally associated with its lace making. Although no longer carried out to its former extent lace making skills are still practised on a much smaller scale. As well as lace Honiton is also famous for its pottery which can be obtained from the pottery shop at the eastern end of the High Street. Honiton also enjoys a reputation as being the antiques centre of the South West, with numerous such shops offering hours of browsing for collectors and enthusiasts alike. The main street ('High Street'), along which the present town centre is broadly based, runs for nearly a mile and is set along part of the route of the Roman road which ran from Dorchester to Exeter. However the original 'centre' of Honiton was in fact high on the hill, to the south of the present town, where the former parish church of St Michael's still stands. Built in the late 15th early 16th century the church's interior was destroyed by a fire in 1911 leaving only the walls and tower standing. The tomb of Thomas Marwood who was a physician to Queen Elizabeth I also survived the fire. Marwood obviously practised what he

Marwood House

preached because he died at the grand old age of 105. It was Marwood's second son John, also a physician, who in 1619 built Marwood House at the eastern end of the High Street. Supposedly visited by Charles II, the property was restored in 1828 and completely modernised in 1930 and is Honiton's oldest remaining residential property.

The oldest building in Honiton however is the Allhallows Museum. This building dates back to around 1230 and was originally built as a chapel by residents who had become weary of the long climb up the hill to St Michael's Church. Since then records indicate that the chapel was also used as a school before being shortened in 1835 to make room for the building of the 'new' parish church of St Pauls alongside. The chapel was purchased by the local townsfolk just over 50 years ago when it became the museum it is today. The museum houses the excavated bones of Hippos who were the town's earliest known dwellers going back over 100,000 years ago. The main exhibit, however, is that of Honiton Lace and it is recognised as the world's most comprehensive collection. Honiton Lace has been a favourite with our Royal Family for many years and the Queen herself had a christening robe which has been used by her children and grandchildren. To this day the Speaker of the House of Commons wears Honiton Lace. Demonstrations of lace making can be seen at the museum daily during June, July and August.

The 104 foot high tower of St Pauls Church is a conspicuous landmark for many miles around and dominates the town's skyline. It was designed in the Norman style by Charles Fowler and the interior of the building was significantly altered in 1987 thus creating space for the Transfiguration Chapel. Honiton was devastated by fires in 1747, 1754 and 1765, the latter claiming over 115 dwellings, and as a result much of the town's early history was destroyed. The rebuilding of Honiton since the fires has resulted in its present appearance of being a fine 18th century Georgian town. It remains an attractive and prosperous town, with excellent shops and facilities and is particularly lively on the days the twice weekly street market is held.

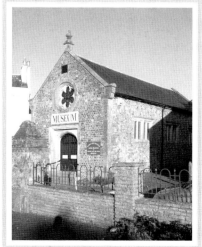

Allhallows Museum

8. WORFIELD HOUSE to WESTON CROSS

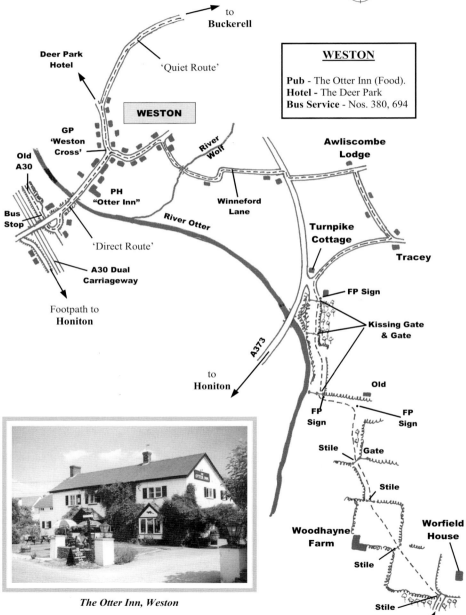

to **Buckerell**

'Quiet Route'

Deer Park Hotel

WESTON

Pub - The Otter Inn (Food).
Hotel - The Deer Park
Bus Service - Nos. 380, 694

WESTON

GP 'Weston Cross'

Old A30

River Wolf

Awliscombe Lodge

PH "Otter Inn"

Winneford Lane

Bus Stop

River Otter

'Direct Route'

Turnpike Cottage

Tracey

A30 Dual Carriageway

FP Sign

Footpath to **Honiton**

Kissing Gate & Gate

A373

to **Honiton**

Old

FP Sign

FP Sign

Stile

Gate

Stile

Woodhayne Farm

Worfield House

Stile

Stile

The Otter Inn, Weston

30

SECTION LENGTH = 1.91 miles (to Weston Cross)

⬤ To the left of the gate of 'Worfield House' there is a stile. Cross this and head diagonally right down the field to another stile. Cross over and then head diagonally across the field to another stile. Cross this and a stream and follow the left-hand field edge to another stile. Go over this and keeping the fence on your right head towards a derelict barn. Just before you get to the barn bear left and head down towards the river. At the river turn right through a kissing gate and go along a track through two more kissing gates and continue on as far as the main road (A373). If you wish to go to Honiton turn left along the main road, and there is a footpath alongside the road all the way to the town centre which is about ¾ mile away. Otherwise just before reaching the main road turn right up the side road (signed 'Egland') to the right of 'Turnpike Cottage'. Follow this road uphill and when you come to an S-bend turn sharp left into a lane. Follow this all the way to a junction near 'Awlicombe Lodge' at the entrance to the drive leading to 'Awliscombe House'. Here turn left and continue on until you come to a junction with the A373 again. Here cross the road, turn right, and then turn immediately left into a lane ('Winneford Lane'). Continue along the lane crossing a ford over the River Wolf. When you reach a road junction turn left and go down through the village of Weston as far as 'Weston Cross'.

There is now a choice of three routes to get to Fenny Bridges; the 'Direct Route' along the former A30, or a 'Quiet Route' along lanes as far as Buckerell and then across fields and the River Otter to join up with the 'Direct Route'. Alternatively you can follow the 'Quiet Route' as far as Buckerell but then continue along lanes to Fenny Bridges in which case the total distance from Weston Cross will be 3.13 miles.

The 'Direct Route'

⬤ From 'Weston Cross' carry straight on down the road past the 'Otter Inn' on your left, and over the River Otter. As you approach the bridge ahead of you, turn left and follow the slip road round to the right and down under the bridge.

The 'Quiet Route'

⬤ If you need refreshments continue on about two hundred yards down the road to the 'Otter Inn' and then retrace your steps back to 'Weston Cross'. Otherwise turn right and follow the road all the way to Buckerell (almost 1½ miles).

Buckerell

General Facilities - Public Telephone Call Box. B&B - Splathayes, Broadlands
Bus service - No 694.
It is thought that the name 'Buckerell' dates from the 13th century when a certain Andrew Bokerel, who was Lord Mayor of London seven times, came to live in the area. The church of St Mary and St Giles has a 14th century tower and contains a monument to Samuel Graves who was the unsuccessful Commander-in-Chief of the British forces involved in the infamous 'Boston Tea Party'.

FENNY BRIDGES

Pub - The Greyhound (B&B & Food).
B&B - Little Ash Farm, Skinners Ash Farm (also teas in summer)
Bus Services - Nos. 382, 387. (Note - Service No 380 serves the old A30 between the railway bridge and Weston turnings)

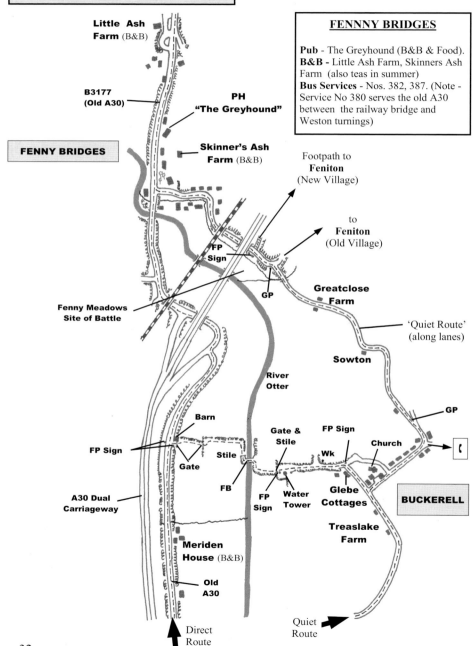

Little Ash Farm (B&B)

B3177 (Old A30)

PH "The Greyhound"

FENNY BRIDGES

Skinner's Ash Farm (B&B)

Footpath to **Feniton** (New Village)

to **Feniton** (Old Village)

FP Sign

Greatclose Farm

GP

'Quiet Route' (along lanes)

Fenny Meadows Site of Battle

Sowton

River Otter

GP

Barn

Gate & Stile

FP Sign

Church

FP Sign

Wk

Stile

Gate

FB

FP Sign

Water Tower

Glebe Cottages

BUCKERELL

A30 Dual Carriageway

Treaslake Farm

Meriden House (B&B)

Old A30

Direct Route

Quiet Route

```
SECTION LENGTHS = 3.13 miles (via Direct Route)
                  4.03 miles (via Quiet Route)
```

Note:- As mentioned in the previous section you can if you wish, continue along lanes from Buckerell to Fenny Bridges (1.78 miles) in which case follow the route shown on the sketch map opposite. (Unfortunately space does not permit descriptive notes)

The 'Quiet Route' (continued)

⓿ **As you approach Buckerell turn left into a lane** ('Cabbage Lane'). **Follow this down past 'Glebe Cottages' and then turn left onto the track. Follow the track down to where it turns right** at a waymark. **At this point you carry on straight ahead and down to a metal gate and stile. Go over the stile into the field and follow the left-hand edge down to the river. At the river cross over the footbridge and then the stile on the other side and turn right to go along the riverbank. At the field boundary turn left and follow it up to a gate beyond which you go onto a track. Follow this up to a barn and turn right onto the road** where you now follow the directions for the 'Direct Route' from the appropriate point indicated below.

The 'Direct Route' (continued)

⓿ **From the bridge go along the old A30** past 'Meriden House' **and continue on until you get to a footpath sign opposite a solitary barn** on the right. This is the point where the 'Quiet Route' joins from your right. **From here continue along the road to its junction with a slip road. Turn right and go along the road (B3177) towards the road bridge. Go under the road bridge and then a railway bridge. Go past two road junctions,** both on your left, one signed to Gittisham and the other to Ottery St Mary (B3177), **and continue along the main road to Fenny Bridges,** crossing bridges over the River Otter and Vine Stream. Fenny Bridges was hit by floods in July 1968 and although the existing brick arched bridge over the Otter built in 1810 by James Green survived, a bridge over the adjoining Vine Stream was destroyed. If you turn right onto the road signed to Feniton and follow this under two bridges you will come to Fenny Meadows where in 1549 an army of rebels from Devon and Cornwall were defeated by government forces led by Lord Russell. Known as the 'Prayer Book Rebellion' the rebels were up in arms against having to use the new Prayer Book. The commemorative stone alongside the site was erected in 2000.

⓿ **For the main walk go past the junction** to Feniton **and continue on the footpath** alongside the main road **past the entrance to 'Skinners Ash Farm' and the 'Greyhound'** public house. Just after the row of houses on your right the footpath ends. You now have to walk on the road again so take great care. **Carry on along the road past 'Little Ash Farm'** on your left, **and continue on for a short distance until you come to a footbridge on your right** which goes over the A30.

Note:- You can if you wish break your journey here. By crossing over the footbridge you will join a footpath which takes you across fields to Feniton (just over 1 mile) with its shops, public house and main line railway station (Exeter to London Waterloo).

10. LITTLE ASH FARM to CADHAY BRIDGE

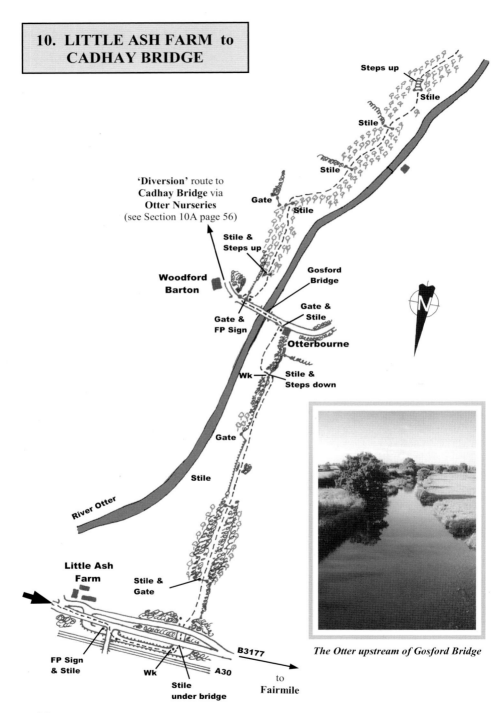

Steps up

Stile

Stile

Stile

'Diversion' route to
Cadhay Bridge via
Otter Nurseries
(see Section 10A page 56)

Gate

Stile

Stile &
Steps up

Gosford
Bridge

**Woodford
Barton**

Gate &
Stile

Gate &
FP Sign

Otterbourne

Wk

Stile &
Steps down

Gate

Stile

River Otter

**Little Ash
Farm**

Stile &
Gate

FP Sign
& Stile

Wk

B3177

Stile
under bridge

A30

to
Fairmile

The Otter upstream of Gosford Bridge

34

⬛ **To continue the walk** do not go across the footbridge but instead **go down the path** which runs between the old and new A30 **and continue ahead** between the two fences. **In a short distance you come to an old railway bridge** on the left. **Go down to a stile under the bridge.** You are now on the track bed of the old LSWR railway line which ran from Sidmouth Junction (now Feniton) to Sidmouth. The line opened on the 6th July 1874. **Cross over the stile and go under the bridge and then under a second bridge and out into a field. Bear slightly right and, keeping the fence on your right, head for a stile and gate ahead of you. Go over the stile and follow the old trackbed** through the copse **to another stile. Cross this and continue** as the embankment gradually reduces in height, **to where it eventually merges into an open field. Keeping the boundary fence on your left follow it towards the**

cottage you will see in the distance. As you near the cottage go left over a stile in the hedge, not through the gate ahead of you, **and down onto the riverbank. Turn right along the riverbank** towards the bridge **and then up to a stile out onto the road**. The building immediately on your right, 'Otterbourne', was formerly the crossing keeper's cottage for the level crossing that used to be here. **For the walk turn left across 'Gosford Bridge'** built in 1824 - 1825 by James Green.

Gosford Bridge

Note:- *At the time of going to print our preferred route to Cadhay Bridge was closed beyond Gosford Bridge due to serious landslips. If this is still the case when you get here, you should follow the 'Diversion' which is included as Section 10A on page 56. In any event this diversion offers both an opportunity to visit Otter Nurseries, where refreshments can be obtained, and also a direct route into Ottery St Mary. If it has been reopened and you wish to continue your walk along the preferred route, you should bear in mind that a re-routing of the footpath will almost certainly have taken place. As a consequence, some of the initial directions given below will no longer apply, although we hope it will be reasonably easy to pick up the original route again.*

⬛ **At the footpath sign** on your right **turn right through a metal gate into the field** alongside the river. **Bearing slightly left away from the river go across some rough ground to some steps up to a stile. Cross over the stile into woods and follow the path along the cliff edge until you come to another stile. Cross over the stile** into a field **and turn right to go along the field edge** with the river down below on your right. **Continue to follow the field edge to a stile. Cross over the stile** and go back into the woods again. **Follow the undulating path through the woods to a another stile. Cross over this and out into the open again before heading back towards the woods to some steps leading up to a stile. Cross over and again follow the path through woods and continue on until it eventually drops down to the river and a footbridge** over a mill leat.

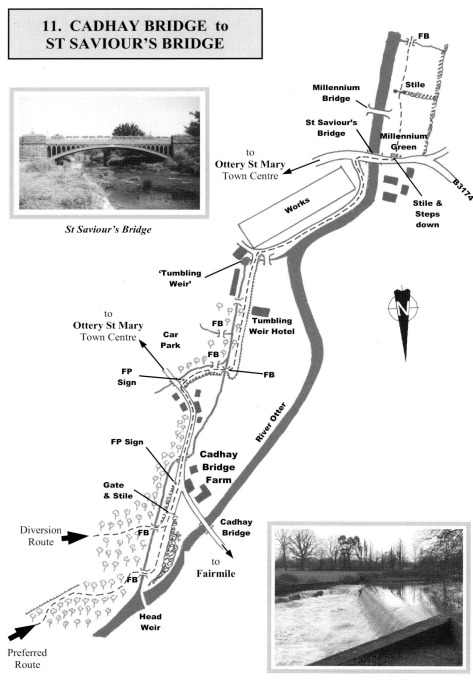

11. CADHAY BRIDGE to ST SAVIOUR'S BRIDGE

St Saviour's Bridge

FB

Millennium Bridge

Stile

St Saviour's Bridge

Millennium Green

to **Ottery St Mary** Town Centre

Works

B3174

Stile & Steps down

'Tumbling Weir'

to **Ottery St Mary** Town Centre

Car Park

FB

Tumbling Weir Hotel

FB

FB

FB

FP Sign

FP Sign

River Otter

Gate & Stile

Cadhay Bridge Farm

Diversion Route

FB

Cadhay Bridge

to **Fairmile**

FB

Head Weir

Preferred Route

The weir upstream of Cadhay Bridge

⬈ **Cross over the bridge and turn left. Follow the right-hand bank of the leat to another footbridge** on your left. This is the point at which the 'Diversion' route via Otter Nurseries rejoins. **Continue to follow the right-hand bank of the leat to a gate and stile. Go over and continue on until you come to the road** at 'Cadhay Bridge Farm'. **Bear left and go along the road** with the mill leat now on the right, **until the road goes round to the left** past some cottages **to a car park** on the right.

If you wish to go to the centre of Ottery St Mary carry straight on, turning left at either the first ('Hind Street') or second ('Mill Street') junction. You can however continue the walk to take in the unusual 'tumbling weir' and another opportunity will then present itself to visit the town centre.

The Tumbling Weir

⬈ **Just before the car park turn right** (signposted) **onto a footpath running alongside a stream. Continue on to a bridge over the mill leat and after crossing over, turn left on the path to go alongside the leat. Go past the 'Tumbling Weir Hotel'** on your right **and continue on until the path reaches the unusual circular Tumbling Weir.** The weir was built in 1790 to provide power for the former serge mills nearby. In the 18th century the mill produced lace until eventually becoming the engineering works that it still is today. The works provides one of the main sources of employment in the town.

At this point you have another opportunity to visit the town centre. Turn left and follow the footpath to where it comes out into 'Mill Street'. Again turn left and follow the footpath alongside the road until it turns left into 'Canaan Way'. At this point cross over to your right into what is still 'Mill Street'. The main square is then only a few hundred yards further along

⬈ **From the tumbling weir** the path bears right and down towards the river **again. Continue alongside the river** between it and the factory **until you come to an open gateway alongside the road bridge,** 'St Saviour's Bridge'. The original four arched bridge was destroyed by floods in 1849 and then replaced by the present structure. **To continue the walk turn right** over the bridge **and then cross the road** to a footpath sign. **Here go down some steps and over a stile** and into what is now Ottery St Mary's 'Millennium Green'. **Follow the river** past a footbridge on your left which was erected in 2001 as part of a project to commemorate the new millennium **and continue on to a stile. Cross the stile and follow the riverbank to a footbridge.**

Ottery St Mary

Early Closing - *Wednesday.* **General Facilities** - *Post Office, Banks, Hotels and B&B's, Shops, Restaurants, Cafes, Library and other such facilities expected to be found in a small country town.* **Pubs** - *The following are in the town centre and all do food:- Lamb & Flag, Kings Arms, London Inn, Volunteer.* **Bus Services** - *Nos. 60, 380, 382, 387, 379.* **Tourist Information Centre** - *in Broad Street, opening times Mondays to Fridays 9.30 - 16.30 and Saturdays a.m. in July & August.*

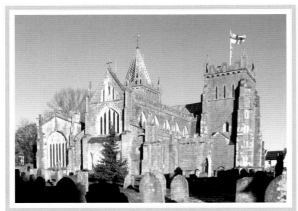

The magnificent Parish Church of Ottery St Mary

Twinned with Pont L'Eveque in Normandy, Ottery St Mary is a small but busy country town which stands on the eastern side of the River Otter in pleasant rural surroundings. Dating back to Saxon times the name 'Ottery' was derived from 'Otrei' the name of the Manor house occupied by the Canons of Rouen (1061-1337) and is mentioned in the Domesday Book in 1086. The suffix 'St Mary' was added in 1207 in honour of the church at Rouen, although in those days it was 'Sca. Maria de Otery'. Ottery's parish church is acknowledged as being one of the finest parish churches in England and dominates the town's skyline. After purchasing the manor and church from Rouen in 1335 it was modified to its present mini Exeter Cathedral appearance from 1337 to 1342 by John de Grandisson who at the time was Bishop of Exeter and was supervising the building of the Cathedral there. At the same time the right to form a college (collegiate) was granted to Grandisson by Edward III thus resulting in Grandisson being able to fulfil a long term wish to form an establishment for learned clerics. The church itself has twin towers, both 64 feet high, with one of them surmounted by a spire. The weather cock on this spire at over six hundred years old is believed to be one of the oldest still in working order. One of the buildings which made up Grandisson's Collegiate was 'Chanters House' which still exists today. It was here that Oliver Cromwell stayed with Sir Thomas Fairfax whilst visiting the town during the English Civil War. Ottery St Mary, like many towns, was not without its

The Stocks in the Churchyard

disastrous fires. The worst of these occurred on 25th May 1866 resulting in the loss of over a hundred properties and five hundred people being made homeless. Remarkably there were hardly any casualties. The fire gutted properties in Jesu Street and Mill Street but was prevented from reaching the mill itself. The Square in Broad Street forms the focal point of the town with its star shaped road pattern being typical of many Saxon Settlements. In 1226

The Square, Broad Street

Henry III granted Ottery a Charter to hold a fair or market. This used to be held at the top of Silver Street / The Flexton where there is now a monument commemorating Queen Victoria's Diamond Jubilee. It was also here that the village stocks were situated, and these can now be seen in the nearby churchyard. No reference to Ottery St Mary would be complete without mentioning its world famous Tar Barrel ceremony which takes place every year on November 5th. Just before dawn the local townsfolk are awakened by the traditional firing of a cannon to mark the start of the days events. Starting in the afternoon with small barrels carried by women and children, these events cumulate in the evening when thousands of people gather in the main streets and square to watch local men carry much larger barrels full of burning tar on their shoulders. This they do for as long as possible and as soon as a barrel becomes 'unbearable' someone else is always on hand to take over. Whilst the origins of the ceremony are unclear it is widely accepted that the tradition dates back to times when it was a common ritual to cleanse the streets of evil spirits.

Samuel Taylor Coleridge

Ottery St Mary's most famous son is undoubtedly Samuel Taylor Coleridge who was born here on October 21st 1772. He was the youngest son of the Reverend John Coleridge, who was the headmaster at the local 'Kynge's Newe Grammar Scole' which was formed in 1645 by Henry VIII. Samuel Coleridge was known to be a daydreamer and this was reflected in much of his work. Many references to Ottery were made in his earlier works but his best known works such as 'The Rime of the Ancient Mariner', 'Kubla Khan' and 'Christabel' were written after meeting the poet William Wordsworth with whom he spent much time in the Lake District. Coleridge died in 1834. A plaque commemorating him can be found on the wall just across from the Jubilee Monument.

For those of you who wish to explore more of this fascinating little town an excellent town trail guide is available from the Tourist Information Centre in Broad Street.

12. ST SAVIOUR'S BRIDGE to TIPTON MILL

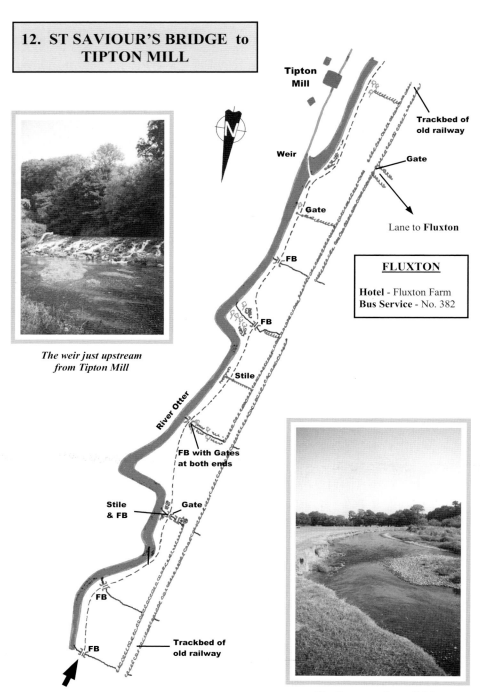

The weir just upstream from Tipton Mill

Tipton Mill

Trackbed of old railway

Weir

Gate

Gate

Lane to **Fluxton**

FB

FB

FLUXTON

Hotel - Fluxton Farm
Bus Service - No. 382

Stile

River Otter

FB with Gates at both ends

Stile & FB

Gate

FB

FB

Trackbed of old railway

The Otter near Ottery St Mary

⬤ Cross this footbridge and continue following the riverbank and then cross another footbridge. After crossing this you can clearly see where the river has altered its course after heavy rain at the end of 2000. **Follow the riverbank until,** when close between the river and the old railway line, **you come to a stile** next to a metal field gate. **Go over the stile into the next field.** The river heads away left but you **continue ahead to where the river is rejoined at the next field boundary. Go over the footbridge** via the gates at either end **and into the next field. Follow the edge of the river to a waymarked stile** in a post and wire fence. **Cross over this into the next field and continue to follow the river** until you come to what in winter can be a very marshy area. **Then** depending on conditions **either head straight across or skirt around the marshy area to the footbridge which is in the field boundary ahead of you. Cross over this and follow the river to another footbridge. Continue to follow the river to a waymarked metal gate** next to a solitary oak tree. **Keep on following the riverbank until you get to a weir** which is the head of the mill leat serving 'Tipton Mill' which you will see on the opposite bank when a little further down the river. **From the weir continue along the river to a gap in the fence** which forms the next field boundary. **Go through and follow the riverbank around towards the old railway viaduct** which goes over the river. This substantial structure is 55 yards long and although near to Tipton St John it was actually known as the 'Ottery St Mary Viaduct'. Do not go up onto the viaduct, but **follow the riverbank underneath it.**

'Ottery St Mary Viaduct' near Tipton St John

41

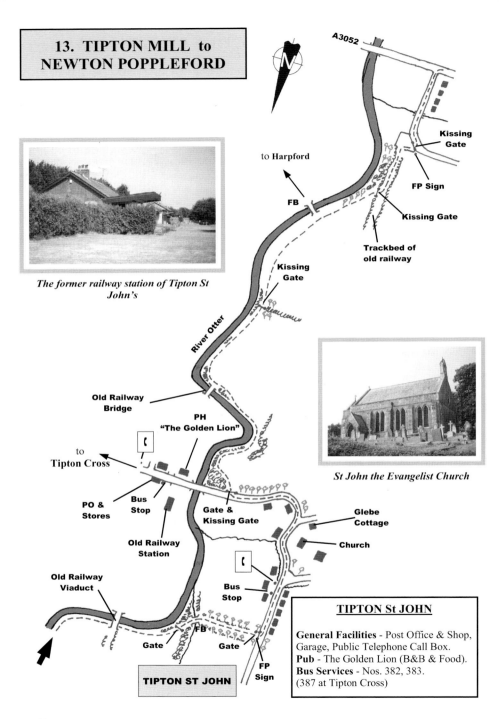

13. TIPTON MILL to NEWTON POPPLEFORD

A3052

to Harpford

Kissing Gate

FP Sign

FB

Kissing Gate

Trackbed of old railway

Kissing Gate

The former railway station of Tipton St John's

River Otter

Old Railway Bridge

PH "The Golden Lion"

to Tipton Cross

St John the Evangelist Church

PO & Stores

Bus Stop

Gate & Kissing Gate

Glebe Cottage

Church

Old Railway Station

Old Railway Viaduct

Bus Stop

FB

Gate

Gate

FP Sign

TIPTON ST JOHN

TIPTON St JOHN

General Facilities - Post Office & Shop, Garage, Public Telephone Call Box.
Pub - The Golden Lion (B&B & Food).
Bus Services - Nos. 382, 383.
(387 at Tipton Cross)

⬤ From the viaduct follow the river round to a wooden gate. Go through this and then immediately right over a concrete footbridge. Go up the track through an avenue of trees **to a gate**. **Go through the gate onto the road and turn left to continue on through the village of Tipton St John,** passing the church of St John the Evangelist. **At the school follow the road round to the left.** Notice the picturesque 'Glebe Cottage' just up the road off to your right. **Follow the main road until you reach a pump house** on the right-hand side. **Immediately after this, but before the river bridge, you will see a gap on your right and a kissing gate.** If you wish to visit Tipton St John or take a refreshment break carry on over the river bridge where the 'Golden Lion' is immediately on the right. **To continue the walk go through the gap and turn left** in the field **to go to the riverbank. Follow the riverbank round the long bend** (not the direct route across the river as shown on the 'Explorer' map!), **and continue on past an old steel railway bridge** on your left. This bridge is on the former branch line from Tipton St John to Budleigh Salterton which opened in 1897 and

Glebe Cottage, Tipton St John

was extended as far as Exmouth in 1903. The line became a victim of the infamous 'Beeching Axe' and closed in March 1967. **Continue to follow the riverbank all the way to a wooden kissing gate in the next hedge. After going through the gate continue alongside the river all the way to a footbridge** ('Harpford Bridge'). This is where the 'East Devon Way' crosses your path and leads to Harpford.

The 'East Devon Way' is a forty mile long inland route which links footpaths, bridleways and country lanes between the Exe at Exmouth and the Lym at Uplyme near the Dorset Boundary. Often known as the 'Foxglove Way', the route goes through a designated area of outstanding natural beauty. An excellent booklet describing the route is available, published by East Devon District Council.

Harpford

In the churchyard is a memorial to the Rev A.M. Toplady who wrote the hymn 'Rock of Ages'. The first verse of the hymn is inscribed on the base of his memorial. Also in the village is 'Harpford House' a grand chateau styled house built by Lord Clinton, a director of the former London & South Western Railway.

⬤ From the bridge continue on along the river until you come to a wooden kissing gate. Go through the gate onto the old railway track and turn left along the trackbed. **Continue on to another kissing gate** and footpath sign next to a metal field gate **and go out onto a road** ('Back Lane'). **Turn left on the road and follow it to its junction with the main A3052 road at Newton Poppleford.**

14. NEWTON POPPLEFORD to WRINKLY CLIFF

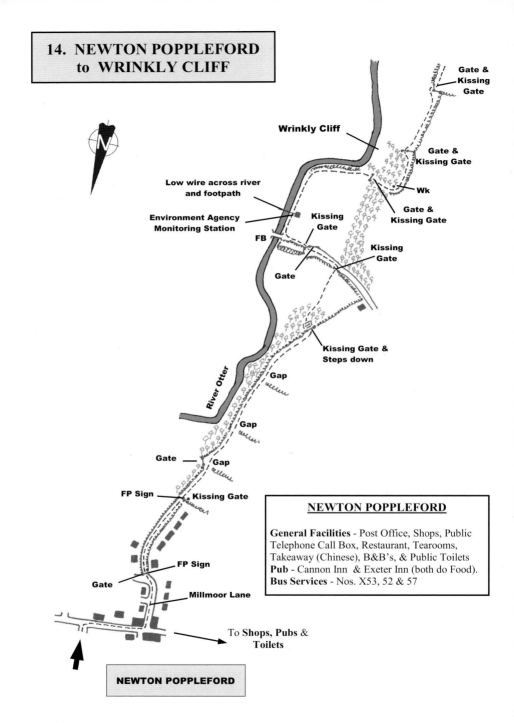

Gate & Kissing Gate

Wrinkly Cliff

Gate & Kissing Gate

Low wire across river and footpath

Wk

Environment Agency Monitoring Station

Gate & Kissing Gate

Kissing Gate

FB

Kissing Gate

Gate

Kissing Gate & Steps down

River Otter

Gap

Gap

Gate

Gap

FP Sign

Kissing Gate

FP Sign

Gate

Millmoor Lane

To **Shops, Pubs** & **Toilets**

NEWTON POPPLEFORD

General Facilities - Post Office, Shops, Public Telephone Call Box, Restaurant, Tearooms, Takeaway (Chinese), B&B's, & Public Toilets
Pub - Cannon Inn & Exeter Inn (both do Food).
Bus Services - Nos. X53, 52 & 57

NEWTON POPPLEFORD

Newton Poppleford

Newton Poppleford as well as having one of the longest names in Devon also claims to be one of the longest villages. The thatched toll house at the western end of the village is believed to be the oldest in Devon, having been built in 1758 for the Exeter Trust. The 'popple' in the name means a smooth round stone or pebble and as 'tun' was the Saxon word for an enclosure it is thought that the full name simply means a 'new field by the pebble ford'. Before the Otter silted up and Otterton was still a sea port, it was possible that small boats were also able to reach Newton Poppleford. Even the keenest gardener is probably unaware that the 'King Alfred' daffodil originated in the village. Now a housing estate appropriately named 'King Alfred Way' the original plot is at the western end of the village near 'Ye Olde Tolle House'.

Cross over the main road and turn right along the footpath and then first left into 'Millmoor Lane'. 'Millmoor Lane', where a silk factory once existed, was originally known as 'Factory Lane'. **Continue along this road until it dips slightly to the left. Between two houses you will see a wooden gate and a footpath sign to its left. As you near the gate** you will see another wooden footpath sign on the right 'Coltaton Raleigh 1½ miles' (no this is not our spelling mistake!). **Go through the gate which leads onto a path** between tall hedges. **Go along this path to a wooden kissing gate** immediately before which a footpath is signed 'Link Path' to the right. **However you continue ahead staying close to the left-hand field edge to go through a gap in the field boundary, and then downhill and up again to the next field boundary. Again there is a gap in the boundary and again you go downhill and up to the next field boundary and another gap.** Soon you get a nice view of the river down to your left as **you continue on until you come to a kissing gate** at the edge of a copse. **Go over this and down some steps into a field. Head right to cross the field to the kissing gate opposite and turn left down the lane** towards the river. Where the lane becomes a narrow overgrown track there is a field gate and signposted kissing gate to your right. **Go through this and turn left towards the river bridge.** Do not go over the bridge but **turn right along the riverbank. Follow the riverbank** watching out for the cable slung across the path just up from a small weir. If you are taller than 5ft 10ins you run the risk of being beheaded! **As you come to a cliff you go through a waymarked kissing gate** alongside a field gate **and then up a slope past a waymarked post.** By some iron railings **turn left up through a cutting. Carry on up until you get to a waymarked kissing gate. Go through into an open field.** A short way along on the left there is a superb view down to the river. **For the walk follow the footpath which continues along the right-hand edge of the field to a waymarked kissing gate.**

The Otter from Wrinkly Cliff

45

15. WRINKLY CLIFF to OTTERTON BRIDGE

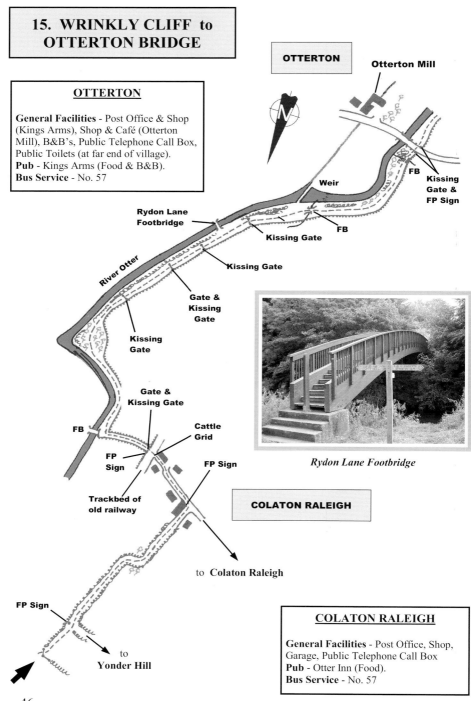

OTTERTON

OTTERTON

General Facilities - Post Office & Shop (Kings Arms), Shop & Café (Otterton Mill), B&B's, Public Telephone Call Box, Public Toilets (at far end of village).
Pub - Kings Arms (Food & B&B).
Bus Service - No. 57

Otterton Mill

FB

Kissing Gate & FP Sign

Weir

FB

Rydon Lane Footbridge

Kissing Gate

Kissing Gate

River Otter

Kissing Gate

Gate & Kissing Gate

Kissing Gate

Gate & Kissing Gate

FB

Cattle Grid

FP Sign

FP Sign

Trackbed of old railway

Rydon Lane Footbridge

COLATON RALEIGH

to **Colaton Raleigh**

FP Sign

to **Yonder Hill**

COLATON RALEIGH

General Facilities - Post Office, Shop, Garage, Public Telephone Call Box
Pub - Otter Inn (Food).
Bus Service - No. 57

46

⬤ **Go through and turn left** with the hedge now on your left-hand side. **You shortly come to the bend of a lane** which to the right goes to Yonder Hill. **For the walk carry on straight ahead** along the 'green lane' and follow this for almost ½ mile **until you get to a road,** ('Church Road').

If you need refreshments or wish to visit the centre of Colaton Raleigh you can turn right up the road, passing 'Place Court' on the way (see notes below), to the junction with the main road, where a short way along on the left, is the Otter Inn.

Colaton Raleigh

The oldest house in the village is 'Place Court' which was built as a rectory or mansion house for the Deans of Exeter Cathedral and has its own chapel. It is in this chapel that Sir Walter Raleigh is reputed to have been baptised. The large gardens of 'Place Court' are surrounded by a long thatched cob wall. Denys Rolle (whose father was Lord Rolle of Bicton) bought the area around the village in 1785.

⬤ **For the walk turn left down the road and go over a cattle grid and the disused railway to a kissing gate. Go through and continue on** towards the river. **At the river** do not cross the footbridge but instead **turn right along the riverbank and follow this all the way to the next wooden kissing gate. Continue to follow the river and go through another two kissing gates and continue on to a curved wooden footbridge which spans the river.** Do not cross the bridge but **continue on through another kissing gate until you come to a weir. From here continue to follow the riverbank and cross a footbridge until just before the road you bear slightly right over a another footbridge crossing a brook and on to a kissing gate** which takes you onto the road at Otterton Bridge that was built by James Green in 1827.

If you wish to go to Otterton, or obtain refreshments, turn left and go over the bridge. 'Otterton Mill' is just over the bridge and further up the road is the 'Kings Arms'.

Otterton

Otterton is regarded as one of those picture postcard villages that visitors to Devon dream of, with its variety of old and new cottages, some dating back to the 15th century. Before the River Otter became

Otterton Bridge

47

16. OTTERTON BRIDGE to WHITE BIDGE

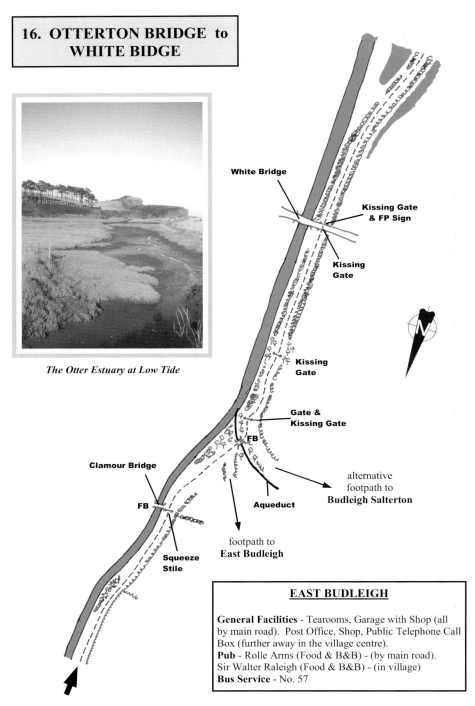

The Otter Estuary at Low Tide

White Bridge

Kissing Gate & FP Sign

Kissing Gate

Kissing Gate

Gate & Kissing Gate

FB

Clamour Bridge

FB

Aqueduct

alternative footpath to
Budleigh Salterton

footpath to
East Budleigh

Squeeze Stile

EAST BUDLEIGH

General Facilities - Tearooms, Garage with Shop (all by main road). Post Office, Shop, Public Telephone Call Box (further away in the village centre).
Pub - Rolle Arms (Food & B&B) - (by main road).
Sir Walter Raleigh (Food & B&B) - (in village)
Bus Service - No. 57

silted up, Otterton was an important seaport under the control of the monks of St Michel in Normandy. They built a small priory in the village and the tower now forms part of the present church of St Michael which was rebuilt in 1870 - 1871. By 1259 the priory belonged to Lord Coleridge of Ottery and in 1539, during the reign of Henry VIII, the Manor was acquired by the Duke family and then subsequently by the Rolle Estates in 1785. The only public house in the village since 1881, 'The Kings Arms' has housed the local Post Office since 1998, although this is not an entirely new occurrence as until the early 1840's mail from all over the lower Otter valley, including Budleigh, was brought here and stamped before being dispatched to Exeter. Otterton Mill was closed in the late 1950's but after renovation it reopened in 1977 as the working mill and craft centre that exists today.

At the Bridge go over the road and down through the kissing gate on the other side **onto the riverbank again. Follow this path** alongside the river **until you get to a squeeze stile. Go through this** and immediately on your left is 'Clamour Bridge' The 'clam' part of the name means a tree trunk which gives a clue as to how at one time the river was probably bridged. **Continue to follow the riverbank to a footbridge** over Budleigh Brook. This brook is carried over the flood plain by means of an aqueduct which was built as part of a land reclaimation project and like many of the fine brick arched bridges along the Otter, was built by James Green. French prisoners of war were used as the labour force for the reclamation project. Just before the aqueduct there is a footpath going off to the right which takes you to the picturesque village of East Budleigh which is well worth a visit if you have time.

East Budleigh

East Budleigh lies on the west side of the River Otter and like Otterton, its neighbour across the river, is a very picturesque and interesting little village attracting many visitors during the summer months. Although there are many fine old buildings to be seen in the village, including All Saints' Church, it is 'Hayes Barton' that is perhaps the best known. Situated to the west of the village it was the birthplace in 1552 of Sir Walter Raleigh. At the time his father, also named Walter, leased the property from Richard Duke. Raleigh spent the first fifteen years of a happy childhood in the area and shortly after being knighted in 1584, he tried unsuccessfully to purchase 'Hayes Barton'. Raleigh's letter, offering to purchase the property, can be seen in the Royal Albert Museum in Exeter. All Saints' Church houses several memorials to the Raleigh family including the family pew with its coat of arms dated 1537.

To continue the walk cross over the footbridge and continue to follow the river going through two kissing gates and then on to another kissing gate at 'White Bridge'. **Cross the road and go through the kissing gate on the other side.** At this point you have entered the Otter Estuary Nature Reserve where several viewing platforms have been situated along the way from which you can observe the immense amount of wildlife on the Estuary.

49

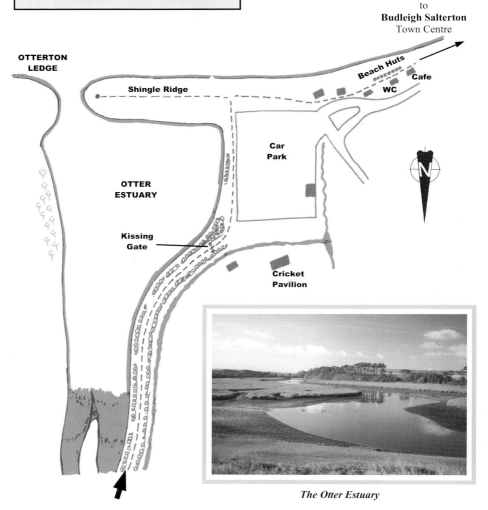

17. WHITE BRIDGE to BUDLEIGH SALTERTON

to
Budleigh Salterton
Town Centre

OTTERTON
LEDGE

Shingle Ridge

Beach Huts

Cafe

WC

Car
Park

OTTER
ESTUARY

Kissing
Gate

Cricket
Pavilion

N

The Otter Estuary

At 'White Bridge' you have joined and will follow part of the 'South West Coast Path' as far as Budleigh Salterton (see notes on the opposite page). **From 'White Bridge' follow the raised footpath alongside the estuary** all the way **to a kissing gate. Go through into the car park and, keeping to the left-hand edge, head for the high shingle ridge ahead of you. When you reach the end of the car park** you can either **turn left and take the lower level path or** you can **go up onto the top of the ridge and turn left and go along the ridge itself.** Either route will lead you to where the Otter enters the sea and . . . . .

JOURNEY'S END.

The 'South West Coast Path' - Over the centuries, fishermen, coastguards and smugglers have contrived to create parts of this historic path. It is Britain's longest national trail and stretches for 630 miles through four counties from Minehead in Somerset right round the South West peninsula to Poole Harbour in Dorset. The path passes along some of the finest coastal scenery in Europe. With its enormous variety and contrast between bustling resort and quiet cove it is a never ceasing source of delight. The path is supported by the South West Coast Path Association, formed in 1973, whose aim is to secure completion of the path as well as its improvement and maintenance. The Association produce an annually updated guide book to the whole length. It contains information about accommodation, camp sites, youth hostels, ferries, tide tables and public transport. Enquiries and details of membership of the Association can be obtained from:- The Administrator, Sarah Vincent, 25 Clobells, South Brent, Devon, TQ10 9JW.

To visit Budleigh Salterton **turn right at the end of the car park and follow the esplanade** alongside the beach huts. The town centre is about ¼ mile further on.

Budleigh Salterton

Early Closing *- Thursday.* ***General Facilities*** *- Post Office, Banks, Hotels and B&B's, Shops, Restaurants, Cafes, Library and other such facilities expected to be found in a seaside resort.* ***Pubs*** *- (All in the town centre and all do food) Salterton Arms, King William VI, Feathers Hotel (B&B).* ***Bus Service*** *- No 57.* ***Tourist Information Centre*** *- in Fore Street* ***Museum*** *- Fairlynch Museum, Fore Street Open: 2.00pm to 4.30pm daily, April to October (and also 11.00am to 13.00pm except Sunday in July and August*

As the name suggests Budleigh Salterton, or Saltern and Salterne as it has been suffixed, takes its name from the salt marshes that used to exist in the area. The salt was used in the preservation of foodstuff and was collected by monks from the nearby Otterton priory. The priory made a good living from this salt production, distributing it via pack animals to many of the

Budleigh Salterton beach and the Otter Estuary beyond

villages sprawled out along the River Otter. The smooth pebbles on the beach are quite large for the East Devon area, and many were believed to have been deposited during the 'Great Storm' of 1824, remaining there to form the present pebble ridge and long stretch of beach. The beach stretches for three miles, and as you walk along the esplanade you are able to enjoy fine panoramic sea views. The view of the town and Lyme Bay from the top of the red sandstone hill at the western end of the town is well worth the climb.

The town itself built up a reputation as a popular coastal holiday town in early Victorian times and much of its character, like many East Devon resorts, remains relatively unspoilt even today. The town centre itself is made up of a fascinating variety of shops and buildings, all of which combine to illustrate the emphasis the town places on conserving its heritage.

The Fairlynch Museum

The Tourist Information Centre is centrally located and nearby is the Fairlynch Museum. Built in 1811 by Matthew Yeates a boatbuilder, the museum is a lovely thatched building and houses exhibitions of the local history of Budleigh Salterton and the Otter Valley as well as costumes and lace. The main displays are changed each year. Across the road from the Museum is the spot on which, in 1870, the Victorian artist Sir John Everett Millais based his famous painting 'The Boyhood of Raleigh'. The ancient wall depicted in the picture is still there today and has an inconspicuous plaque on it where the young Walter is depicted as sitting. The picture was created in the 'Octagon', built in 1818 and a blue plaque has also been erected on the wall of that building. The original painting can usually be seen at the Tate Gallery in London but was 'returned home' for display in the museum during the 2000 season.

BIBLIOGRAPHY

The following books were either useful sources of reference or make recommended reading. With so many books available the list is not intended to be definitive, but merely a small selection of those we came across during our research.

HOSKINS, W.G.	*DEVON.*	DAVID & CHARLES, 1972
PAGE, J.L.W.	*THE RIVERS OF DEVON.*	SEELEY AND CO.LTD, 1893
WILLS, G.	*DEVON ESTUARIES.*	DEVON BOOKS, 1992
BARBER, C.	*ALONG THE OTTER*	OBELISK PUBLICATIONS, 1996
WHITHAM, J.	*OTTERY ST MARY*	PHILLIMORE & CO LTD, 1984
WEBBER, R.	*THE DEVON & SOMERSET BLACKDOWNS*	R. HALE & CO, 1976
DRURY-BECK, M.	*HANDBOOK AND GUIDE TO THE BLACKDOWN HILLS*	MDB LITEWORK, 1999
MILLINGTON, G. & JONES, R.H.	*ALL ABOUT THE OTTER*	KEVEREL PRESS, 2000

PART 4
USEFUL INFORMATION

Tourist Information Centres

Taunton	The Library, Paul Street, Taunton,	01823 336334
Honiton	Lace Walk Car Park, Honiton, EX14 8LT	01404 43716
Ottery St Mary	10b, Broad Street, Ottery St Mary, EX11 1BZ	01404 813964
Budleigh Salterton	Police Station, Fore Street, Budleigh Salterton, EX14 8LT	01395 445275

District Councils

East Devon	The Knowle, Station Road, Sidmouth, Devon, EX10 8HL	01395 516551
Taunton Deane	Deane House, Belvedere Rd, Taunton, Somerset, TA1 1HE	01823 356356

Environment

AA Weatherwatch	09003 401923		*MetOffice(South West)*	09003 444932
Weathercall	Devon – 0891 50504		Somerset – 0891 50505	
Environment Agency	General Enquiries	0645 333111		
Environment Agency	Emergency for reporting environmental incidents		0800 807060	

Taxis

National Taxi Hotline		0800 654321
Heymock	Allens	01823 680708
Honiton	Acorn	01404 41418 / 0800 0282096
	Alpha	01404 41622
	Knights	01404 46910 / 43775
	Mercury	01404 44713
	Pals	01404 43534
Fenny Bridges	Horseshoe	01404 850800 / 0800 3285080
Ottery St Mary	Otter Cabs	01404 812471
Newton Poppleford	Ist Choice	01395 567969
Exmouth	Abacus	01395 222222
(Budleigh Salterton)	AJ's	01395 222655
	Allied	01395 264188
	A-2-B	01395 2239991
	Apollo	01395 224500
	Aquilla	01395 272281
	Budget	01395 266131
	Coastal	01395 272327
	Daves	01395 223333
	Delphi	01395 269474
	Direct	01395 224255
	Discount	01395 223311
	Estuary	01395 223556
	Exmouth	01395 227588
	Freefone	0800 0964433
	Moorfield	01395 222268
	Phils	01395 224133
	Steves	01395 222067
	Swift	01395 222277

Public Transport (Enquiries)

Devon Bus Enquiry Line		01392 382800
Somerset Bus Enquiry Line/ATMOS		01823 358299
Public Transport Traveline		0870 6082608
National Rail Enquiries		08457 484950
National Express Coach Services		08705 808080
First Southern National	Bus Station, Taunton, TA1 4AF	01823 272033
Stagecoach Devon	Bus Station, Paris Street, Exeter, EX1 2JP	01392 427711
Royal Mail Post Bus	The Post Office, High Street, Honiton, EX14 8PA	01404 42001
Cook Coaches	Whiteball Garage, Wellington, TA21 0LT	01823 673155
South West Trains		023 8021 3600

Public Transport (Bus Services)

The following services were available at the time of going to press but you should check the current status with the operator or council enquiry line as they are liable to change without much notice. Also not all services use the "route number" particularly the once a week and County Council supported services.

No	Operator	Frequency	Route
20	First Southern National	Weekdays	Seaton-**Honiton-Combe Raleigh**-Dunkeswell-Hemyock-Taunton.
X53	First Southern National	Weekdays	Exeter-**Newton Poppleford**-Sidford-Seaton-Lyme Regis-Bridport.
52	Stagecoach Devon	Daily	Exeter-**Newton Poppleford**-Sidmouth-Sidbury.
57	Stagecoach Devon	Daily	Exeter-Exmouth-**Budleigh Salterton-East Budleigh-Otterton-Colaton Raleigh-Newton Poppleford**-Sidmouth. Note : Only Exeter-Budleigh Salterton on Sundays in Winter.
60	Stagecoach Devon	Weekdays	Exeter-**Ottery St Mary**-Otter Nurseries.
340	Stagecoach Devon	Weekdays	Sidmouth-Sidbury-Sidford-**Honiton**.
379	Stagecoach Devon	Summer Sunday	Exeter-**Ottery St Mary-Honiton**-Sidbury-Sidmouth.
380	Stagecoach Devon	Weekdays	Exeter-**Ottery St Mary-Alfington-Honiton**-Axminster.
382	Stagecoach Devon	Weekdays	Sidmouth-**Tipton St John-Fluxton-Ottery St Mary-Fenny Bridges-Feniton**-Whimple.
383	Cooks Coaches	Fridays	**Tipton St John**-Exeter.
387	Stagecoach Devon	Mon to Fri	Sidmouth-**Tipton Cross-Ottery St Mary-Honiton-Rawridge-Upottery-Churchinford**-Taunton.
387	Stagecoach Devon	Saturday	Whimple-**Feniton-Honiton-Rawridge-Upottery-Churchinford**-Taunton.
682	Cooks Coaches	Tuesdays	**Honiton-Upottery-Rawridge-Honiton.**
683	Royal Mail Post Bus	Mon to Friday	**Honiton-Combe Raleigh-Upottery-Rawridge-Beacon-Honiton** (Afternoons only)
694	Cooks Coaches	Weekdays	**Feniton-Buckerell-Weston-Honiton.**

Public Transport (Rail Services)

South West Trains	Daily	London (Waterloo) to Exeter service serves **Feniton & Honiton.**

Accommodation

(Note: This list is not comprehensive but just some we have noticed along or near the route. The places listed can range from B&B to 5* Hotels. The list was correct at the time of going to press but things can change rapidly. If in doubt accommodation can be booked through the local Tourist Information Centres at Taunton, Honiton, Ottery St Mary and Budleigh Salterton.

Lower Luxton Farm	near Churchinford	01823 601269
York Inn	Churchinford	01823 601333
Courtmoor Farm	Upottery	01404 861565
Bidwell Farm	Upottery	01404 861122
Robins Cottage	Upottery	01404 861281
The Forge	Upottery	01404 861420
Sidmouth Arms	Upottery	01404 861252
The Pheasantry	Combe Raleigh	01404 42130
Ellishayes Farm	Combe Raleigh	01404 47365
Oaklands	Honiton	01404 44282
The Heathfield	Honiton	01404 45321
New Dolphin Hotel	Honiton	01404 42377
Honiton Motel	Off A30 near Weston	01404 43440
Meriden House	On old A30 near Weston	01404 44155
Roebuck Farm	Weston	01404 42225
Deer Park Hotel	Weston	01404 42064
Broadlands	Buckerell	01404 850894
Splathayes	Buckerell	01404 850464
Jenirens Farm	Buckerell	01404 850274
Skinners Ash Farm	Fenny Bridges	01404 850231
The Greyhound	Fenny Bridges	01404 850380
Little Ash Farm	Fenny Bridges	01404 850271
Pitt Farm	Fairmile	01404 812439
Fairmile Inn	Fairmile	01404 812827
Tumbling Weir Hotel	Ottery St Mary	01404 812752
Normandy House	Ottery St Mary	01404 811088
Salston Manor Hotel	Ottery St Mary	01404 815581
Fluxton Farm Hotel	Nr Tipton St John	01404 812818
Golden Lion	Tipton St John	01404 812881
Higher Coombe Farm	Tipton St John	01404 813385
Peeks Guest House	Harpford	01395 567664
Southern Cross	Newton Poppleford	01395 568439
Burnthouse Farm	near Colaton Raleigh	01395 568304
Kings Arms	Otterton	01395 568416
Wynards Farm	East Budleigh	01395 443417
The King William	Budleigh Salterton	01395 442075
Willowmead	Budleigh Salterton	01395 443115
Long Range Hotel	Budleigh Salterton	01395 443321
Chapel Cottage	Budleigh Salterton	01395 443800
Apple Tree Cottage	Budleigh Salterton	01395 444066
Glendale	Budleigh Salterton	01395 443565
Bay Cottage	Budleigh Salterton	01395 443762
Rosehill	Budleigh Salterton	01395 444031

Amendments since first Publication

Page 27:	**Combe Raleigh** - The reference to The Abbot's House should read "the house known as 'Abbots' was used as a prisoner of war camp in WWI" (not WWII)
Page 28:	**Allhallows Museum, Honiton.** Opening times are now 0930 to 1630 Monday to Friday (closes 1530 in October) and 0930 to 1300 on Saturdays, from Easter to the end of October.
Page 34 & 36:	References to a 'Diversion Route' on the maps are no longer relevant
Page 35:	The preferred route to Cadhay Bridge has now reopened without any re-routing of the original footpath being necessary. You may however still wish to continue along the road to visit Otter Nurseries and then return to Gosford Bridge again to continue the walk. Because there has been no re-routing of the path, the walking notes at the bottom of the page are still relevant.
Page 40:	There is now a footbridge across the river at Tipton Mill allowing circular walks on both sides of the river from either Ottery St. Mary or Tipton St. John.
Page 44:	The Bus Services at Newton Poppleford are now Nos 52, X53 and 157.
Page 46 & 48:	The Bus Service at Colaton Raleigh, Otterton and East Budleigh is now No 157
Page 51:	The Bus Services at Budleigh Salterton are now Nos 157 and 357.

Page 53: **Tourist Information Centres**
Budleigh Salterton TIC's address is:- Fore Street, Budleigh Salterton, EX9 6NG

Taxis:

Delete	Honiton	Acorn	
	Exmouth	Freefone	
Amend	Exmouth	A2B	(Tel No should be 01395 223999)
Add	Honiton	Aries	01404 549892
	Exmouth	Jackson	01395 223868

Page 54: **Public Transport (Enquiries)**
First Southern National is now First in Somerset and Avon
Stagecoach Devon's address is now Belgrave Road, Exeter, EX1 2LB
The Royal Mail Postbus no longer operates
Cook Coaches should be Cook<u>s</u> Coaches and the Tel No is 01823 672247

Public Transport (Bus Services)

Delete	Services 57 and 683
Amend	Service X53 now runs daily and continues to Poole with some services terminating at Bournemouth
Add	

No	Operator	Frequency	Route
157	Stagecoach Devon	Weekdays	Exmouth-**Budleigh Salterton-East Budleigh-Otterton-Colaton Raleigh-Newton Poppleford-**Sidmouth
357	Stagecoach Devon	Weekdays	Exmouth-Budleigh Salterton

Page 55: **Accommodation**
Delete   The Fairmile Inn